Model Test Papers

ICSE Class 10

For Term 2

COMPUTER APPLICATION

Author:
Mr. Mohit Tripathi

Title : Model Test Papers for class -X Computer Application

Author Name : Mr. Mohit Tripathi

Published By : EduGorilla Community Pvt. Ltd.

Publishers Address : 12/651, First Floor Opp. Arvindo Park, Near Jama Masjid, Indira Nagar, Lucknow, Uttar Pradesh - 226016, India

Copyright

ISBN: 9789355563286

Disclaimer

Although the author and publisher have made every effort to ensure the occuracy of information in this book, we do not assume any responsibility to errors and hereby disclaim any liability to any party for any loss, damage, or disruption caused by errors or omissions, whether such errors or omissions result from negligence, accident, or any other cause.

Compiled and Created by EduGorilla Book Experts

Printed by EduGorilla Community Pvt. Ltd.

SYLLABUS

COMPUTER APPLICATION (86)

BIFURCATED SYLLABUS
(As per the Reduced Syllabus for ICSE – Class X Year 2022 Examination)

SEMESTER 2
(Marks: 50)

UNIT NO.	NAME OF THE UNIT
1.	**Using Library Classes** (Complete Unit)
2.	**Encapsulation** (Complete Unit)
3.	**String Handling** (Complete Unit)
4.	**Arrays (Subscripted Variable)** (Complete Unit)
5.	**Exception Handling** (Complete Unit)

COMPUTER APPLICATIONS (86)

CLASS X

*There will be **one** written paper of **two hours** duration carrying 100 marks and Internal Assessment of 100 marks.*

The paper will be divided into two sections A and B.

***Section A (Compulsory** – 40 marks) will consist of compulsory short answer questions covering the entire syllabus.*

***Section B** (60 marks) will consist of questions which will require detailed answers. There will be a choice of questions in this section*

THEORY – 100 Marks

1. Revision of Class IX Syllabus

(i) Introduction to Object Oriented Programming concepts, (ii) Elementary Concept of Objects and Classes, (iii) Values and Data types, (iv) Operators in Java, (v) Input in Java, (vi) Mathematical Library Methods, (vii) Conditional constructs in Java, (viii) Iterative constructs in Java.

2. Class as the Basis of all Computation

Objects and Classes

Objects encapsulate state and behaviour – numerous examples; member variables; attributes or features. Variables define state; member methods; Operations/methods/messages/ methods define behaviour.
Classes as abstractions for sets of objects; class as an object factory; primitive data types, composite data types. Variable declarations for both types; difference between the two types. Objects as instances of a class.
Consider real life examples for explaining the concept of class and object.

3. User - defined Methods

Need of methods, syntax of methods, forms of methods, method definition, method calling, method overloading, declaration of methods,

Ways to define a method, ways to invoke the methods – call by value [with programs] and call by reference [only definition with an example],

Object creation - invoking the methods with respect to use of multiple methods with different names to implement modular programming, using data members and member methods, Actual parameters and formal parameters, Declaration of methods - static and non-static, method prototype / signature, - Pure and impure methods,
- pass by value [with programs] and pass by reference [only definition with an example], Returning values from the methods , use of multiple methods and more than one method with the same name (polymorphism - method overloading).

4. Constructors

Definition of Constructor, characteristics, types of constructors, use of constructors, constructor overloading.
Default constructor, parameterized constructor, constructor overloading., Difference between constructor and method.

5. Library classes

Introduction to wrapper classes, methods of wrapper class and their usage with respect to numeric and character data types. Autoboxing and Unboxing in wrapper classes.

Class as a composite type, distinction between primitive data type and composite data type or class types. Class may be considered as a new data type created by the user, that has its own functionality. The distinction between primitive and composite types should be discussed through examples. Show how classes allow user defined types in programs. All primitive types have corresponding class wrappers. Introduce Autoboxing and Unboxing with their definition and simple examples.

The following methods are to be

covered:

int parseInt(String s),

long parseLong(String s),
float parseFloat(String s),

double parseDouble(String

s),

boolean isDigit(char ch),

boolean isLetter(char ch),

boolean isLetterOrDigit(char

ch), boolean isLowerCase(char

ch), boolean isUpperCase(char

ch), boolean isWhitespace(char

ch), char toLowerCase (char

ch)

char toUpperCase(char ch)

6. Encapsulation

Access *modifiers* and its scope and visibility.

Access modifiers – private, protected and public. Visibility rules for private, protected and public access modifiers. Scope of variables, class variables, instance variables, argumentvariables, local variables.

7. Arrays

Definition of an array, types of arrays, declaration, initialization and accepting data of single dimensional array, accessing the elements of single dimensional array.

Arrays and their uses, Search techniques – linear search and binary search, Array as a composite type, length statement to find the size of the array (searching techniques using single dimensional array only).

8. String handling

String class, methods of String class, implementation of String class methods, String array

The following String class methods are to be covered:
String trim ()
String

toLowerCase()

String

toUpperCase() int

length( )

char charAt (int

n) int

indexOf(char ch)

int lastIndexOf(char ch)

String concat(String

str) boolean equals

(String str)

boolean equalsIgnoreCase(String

str) int compareTo(String str)

int compareToIgnoreCase(String str)

String replace (char oldChar,char

newChar) String substring (int

beginIndex)

String substring (int beginIndex, int

endIndex) boolean startsWith(String str)

boolean endsWith(String

str) String valueOf(all

types)

Programs based on the above methods, extracting and modifying characters of a string, searching for a string using linear search technique.

INTERNAL ASSESSMENT - 100 Marks

This segment of the syllabus is totally practical oriented. The accent is on acquiring basic programming skills quickly and efficiently.

Programming Assignments (Class X)

The students should complete a minimum of 20 laboratory assignments during the whole year to reinforce the concepts studied in class.

Suggested list of Assignments:

The laboratory assignments will form the bulk of the course. Good assignments should have problems which require design, implementation and testing. They should also embody one or more concepts that have been discussed in the theory class. A significant proportion of the time has to be spent in the laboratory. Computing can only be learnt by doing.

The teacher-in-charge should maintain a record of all the assignments done by the student throughout the year and give it due credit at the time of cumulative evaluation at the end of the year.

Some sample problems are given below as examples. The problems are of varying levels of difficulty:

(i) User defined methods

(a) Programs depicting the concept of pure, impure, static, non- static methods.

(b) Programs based on overloaded methods.

(c) Programs involving data members, member methods invoking the methods with respect to the object created.

(ii) Constructors

(a) Programs based on different types of constructors mentioned in the scope of the syllabus.

(b) Programs / outputs based on constructor overloading

(iii) Library classes

(a) Outputs based on all the methods mentioned in the scope of the syllabus.

(b) Programs to check whether a given character is an uppercase/ lowercase / digit etc.

(iv) Encapsulation

Questions based on identifying the different variables like local, instance, arguments, private, public, class variable etc.

(v) Arrays

(a) Programs based on accessing the elements of an array.

(b) Programs based on search techniques mentioned in the scope of the syllabus.

(vi) String handling

(a) Outputs based on all the string methods mentioned in the scope of the syllabus.

(b) Programs based on extracting the characters from a given string and manipulating the same.

(c) Palindrome string, pig Latin, alphabetical order of characters, etc.

Important: This list is indicative only. Teachers and students should use their imagination to create innovative and original assignments.

EVALUATION

The teacher-in-charge shall evaluate all the assignments done by the student throughout the year [both written and practical work]. He/she shall ensure that most of the components of the syllabus have been used appropriately in the assignments. Assignments should be with appropriate list of variables and comment statements. The student has to mention the output of the programs.

Proposed Guidelines for Marking

The teacher should use the criteria below to judge the internal work done. Basically, four criteria are being suggested: class design, coding and documentation, variable description and execution or output. The actual grading will be done by the teacher based on his/her judgment. However, one possible way: divide the outcome for each criterion into one of 4 groups: excellent, good, fair/acceptable, poor/unacceptable, then use numeric values for each grade and add to get the total.

Class design:

Has a suitable class (or classes) been used?
Are all attributes with the right kinds of types present? Is encapsulation properly done?
Is the interface properly designed?

Coding and documentation:

Is the coding done properly? (Choice of names, no unconditional jumps, proper organization of conditions, proper choice of loops, error handling, code layout) Is the documentation complete and readable? (class documentation, variable documentation, method documentation, constraints, known bugs - if any).

Variable description:

Format for variable description:

Name of the Variable	Data Type	Purpose/description

Execution or Output:

Does the program run on all sample input correctly?

Evaluation of practical work will be done as follows:

Subject Teacher (Internal Examiner)	50 marks
External Examiner	50 marks

Criteria (Total-50 marks)	Class design (10 marks)	Variable description (10 marks)	Coding and Documentation (10 marks)	Execution OR Output (20 marks)
Excellent	10	10	10	20

Good	8	8	8	16
Fair	6	6	6	12
Poor	4	4	4	8

An External Examiner shall be nominated by the Head of the School and may be a teacher from the faculty, but not teaching the subject in the relevant section/class. For example, A teacher of Computer Science of class VIII may be deputed to be the External Examiner for class X.

The total marks obtained out of 100 are to be sent to the Council by the Head of the school.

The Head of the school will be responsible for the online entry of marks on the Council's CAREERS portal by the due date.

EQUIPMENT

There should be enough computer systems to provide for a teaching schedule where at least three-fourth of a time available is used for programming and assignments/practical work. The course shall require at least 4 periods of about 40 minutes duration per week. In one week, out of 4 periods the time should be divided as follows:

- 2 periods – Lecture cum demonstration by the instructor.
- 2 periods – Assignments/Practical work.

The hardware and software platforms should be such that students can comfortably develop and run programs on those machines.

Since hardware and software evolve and change very rapidly the schools shall need to upgrade them as required. Following are the minimal specifications as of now.

RECOMMENDED FACILITIES:

- A lecture cum demonstration room with a MULTIMEDIA PROJECTOR/ an LCD and Overhead Projector (OHP) attached to the computer.
- A white board with white board markers should be available.
- A fully equipped Computer Laboratory that allows one computer per student.
- The computers should have a minimum of 1 GB RAM and at least a P - IV or Equivalent Processor.
- Good Quality printers.
- A scanner, a web cam/a digital camera (Shouldbe provided if possible).

SOFTWARE FOR CLASSES IX & X

Any suitable Operating System can be used.

For teaching fundamental concepts of computing using object oriented approach, Blue J environment (3.2 or higher version) compatible with JDK (5.0 or higher version) as the base or any other editor or IDE, compatible with JDK (5.0 or higher version) as the base may be used. Ensure that the latest versions of software are used.

How To Prepare

Being Smart in the Exam Center – Some Important Advice

So, you have in all 100 minutes (10 minutes reading time + 90 minutes for writing the answers). You must make good use of the 10 minutes you are allotted for reading the question paper. No, I don't mean by this that you read the question paper 3-4 times.

When you get the paper. Turn to Section B and go through the programs first. Decide 4 programs you are going to attempt. It will take hardly 5 minutes to conclude.

Next, start reading Section A. As and when you get questions whose answer is among one of the four options, quickly make up the answer in your mind. Do this for the output questions as well.

So, when this 10-minute finishes you will have most of the questions solved mentally.

Now you have 90 minutes in your hand. Start from Section A onwards. Don't waste time and be quick. Complete Section A in 15 – 20 minutes. Now don't panic. This is no big deal as the questions are easy and require a tick only. Yes, I know YOU can.

You will have more than 60 minutes left with you (if you took approx. 30 minutes for section – A). Start writing the programs.

Don't waste time in writing detailed comments or data descriptions. Just a few lines (4 to 6 comments and 5 or 6 lines in data description) will be sufficient. It hardly matters. But don't skip writing them.

Now I would suggest you attempt all the 6 questions if you know. Only the best 4 are selected. So, if you attempt 6 questions in 60 minutes, which comes to around 10 to 15 minutes per program. Which I think is enough. If you cannot attempt 6 questions, then at least attempt 5 questions, and if possible do it in order.

Don't forget to take a look at the whole paper at last. So, manage your time to save at least 5 to 10 minutes for that.

What to cover for the theory part?

Now in this portion, you get questions from all parts of your syllabus (reduced). So, you need to go through your notes for a brief theory of every chapter.

Remember, In MCQs, questions can ask from any type. Give importance to the various Character, String and Mathematical functions.

I have tried to list down few of the important topics from the theory part which should be taken into consideration while going through the theory part. Here I also mentioned some topics from Term – 1. Since there is no chance to come anything from Term – 1 directly but topics will be used in writing programs, outputs. So, it is better to have a recap for few topics from Term – 1.

- Classes as abstractions for sets of objects; class as an object factory; concept of type, primitive data types, composite data types. Variable declarations for both types; difference between the two types. Objects as an instances of a class.
- Tokens and types (Keyword, identifier, literal, operator, separator/punctuator).
- Operators – types and calculations using pre-fix or post-fix
- Data types and their size, range.
- Type Conversion – implicit, explicit
- Writing java expression for a given equation.
- Loops (while, do while and for), nested loops, break and continue.
- Access specifiers and scope and visibility
- Scope of variables, instance variables, argument variables, local variables.
- Class as a composite type, distinction between primitive type and composite or class types.
- Class may be considered as a new data type created by the user, that has its own functionality.
- Wrapper class.

ICSE X
Computer Application

1 USING LIBRARY CLASSES

1.1 Library classes: As library means collection of so many things. Library classes simply means collection of pre – defined classes in java which get included in an application program itself. They are also called **standard java classes or built – in java classes**. These classes also have built in member variables, constructors and methods like ordinary user/programmer's defined classes. These library classes are contained in packages.

Remark:
(i) Name of a class always starts with a capital letter.
(ii) Name of a method/function always start with a small letter and have ( ).

1.2. Packages: Initially it is a group of classes. It is also termed as **Java class library**. The classes contained in packages can be reused in other programs by importing them. Examples of some packages are java.utll, java.io, java.lang etc.

1.3. Import: Whenever a function needs to be used. It can be used just by importing the package, which contains the class, in which the required function present.
import is the keyword which is used to include a package in programs. Syntax for importing a package is following:
import package1.package2.classname (or *);

For Example:
import java.util.Scanner – import specially Scanner class into the current program.
import java.util.* - import all (* means all) classes stored in util package.
Note: All of the standard java classes include with java are stored in a package called java.
lang is a default package which is by default imported in java. So it is useless to write import java.lang.*.

1.4. Wrapper classes: The Wrapper classes in java provides the mechanism to converting primitive/fundamental data types into objects. For example Character is the wrapper class for char, Integer is the wrapper class for int etc. All wrapper classes are part of java.lang package.

Syntax to convert primitive type in to object using wrapper classes:
<class name> <object name> = new <class name>(value);
For example:
```
int  a = 5;                    // a, which is primitive type, contains 5
Integer ob = new Integer(a);   //ob, which is reference type, contains 5
System.out.println(a + "\t" + ob);
```
Output: 5   5
Primitive data types with their wrapper classes

Primitive Data types	Wrapper class
char	Character
byte	Byte

short	Short
long	Long
Int	Integer
float	Float
double	Double
boolean	Boolean

Advantage/use of wrapper classes:

(i) Wrapper classes enables a primitive value to be used as an object.

(ii) Primitive types are passed by value, but objects are passed by reference, so using wrapper classes primitive values can be pass as reference.

1.5 The parse... method: This method converts a valid string representation of a number into corresponding numeric type. Every class has its own type **parse** method. **Integer** class has **paseInt( )** method, **Float** class has **parseFloat( )**, **Double** class has **parseDouble( )** method and so on.

parseInt( ) method converts a valid string representation into **int** type, **parseDouble( )** converts a valid string representation into **double** and so on.

For Example:

int num = Integer.parseInt("25");
double val = Double.parseDouble("6.5");
System.out.println(num*2);
System.out.println(val*2);

Output: 50
13.0

1.6 The Character class: As we know that the **Character** class is a wrapper class for the primitive datatypes **char** and it wraps a value of **char** into an object. This class contains several methods, some important methods are discussed here in the table with syntax and example. Prepare them well for output questions.

Methods/functions of Character class:

S. No.	Functions with their return type	Description	Example
1.	boolean isLetter(char ch)	It returns true if character stored in ch is a letter, otherwise returns false. Return type : **boolean**	char ch = 'a'; boolean b =Character.isLetter(ch); so b = true
2.	boolean isLetterOrDigit(ch)	It returns true if character stored in ch is a letter or digit, otherwise returns false. Return type : **boolean**	char ch = '5'; boolean b =Character.isLetterOrDigit(ch); so b= true
3.	boolean isLowerCase(char ch)	It returns true if character stored in ch is a	char ch = 'A';

		lowercase/small letter, otherwise returns false. Return type : **boolean**	boolean b =Character.isLowerCase(ch); so b = false
4.	boolean isUpperCase(char ch)	It returns true if character stored in ch is a uppercase/capital letter, otherwise returns false. Return type : **boolean**	char ch = 'A'; boolean b =Character.isUpperCase(ch); so b = true

5.	boolean isWhitespace(char ch)	It returns true if character stored in ch is a space/blank, otherwise returns false.
		Return type : **boolean**
			char ch = ' ', ch1='p';
			boolean b =Character.isWhitespace(ch);
			boolean b1 =Character. isWhitespace (ch1);
			so b = true
			and b1 = false

6.	char toUpperCase (char ch)	It converts and returns character stored in ch in uppercase or capital letter if it is a small alphabet, otherwise returns the same value stored in ch.
		Return type: **char**
			char ch = 'a', ch1 = '2';
			char a=Character.toUpperCase(ch);
			char b=Character.toUpperCase(ch1);
			so value of a = 'A'
			and value of b = '2'

7.	char toLowerCase (char ch)	It converts and returns character stored in ch in lowercase or small letter if it is a capital alphabet, otherwise returns the same value stored in ch.
		Return type: **char**
			char ch = 'T', ch1 = '&';
			char a=Character.toLowerCase(ch);
			char b=Character.toLowerCase(ch1);
			so value of a = 't'
			and value of b = '&'

1.7. Autoboxing: The process of automatically converting a primitive type to its corresponding wrapper class object is called **autoboxing**. For example, converting an **int** to an **Integer**, a **double** to a **Double** and so on.

Example of autoboxing:

```
char ch = 'p';
Character ob = ch;      //convert primitive into reference
```

1.8. Unboxing: Converting an object of a wrapper class to its corresponding primitive value is called Unboxing. For example, conversion of Integer to int, Double to double and so on.

Example of unboxing:

```
Integer ob = new Integer (15);
int num = ob;           //convert reference into primitive
```

1.9. Data types: In java we have different types of data, i.e. 2, '2', "2", 2.0 etc. To deal with such type of data java provides a variety of data types. For example, int, double, float etc.

(i) There are 8 primitive or fundamental data types. They are byte, short, int, long, float, double, char and boolean.

(ii) Classes, arrays, interfaces etc. are reference type of data type types in java. They are used to store reference type values.

Java data types are of two types—

1. **Primitive:** It comes as a part of the language and loaded in memory as soon as program loaded. It is also termed as pre-defined, intrinsic or fundamental data types. For ex. int, byte, double etc.
2. **Non primitive or derived or reference:** These types are formed with the help of primitive type. Arrays and classes/objects are of reference type.

Input/Output statements in java-

- **Take Input using BufferedReader in various Data types:**

  BufferedReader br=new BufferedReader(new InputStreamReader(System.in));

  For interger:

  int a=Integer.parseInt(br.readLine());

  For short:

  short a= Short.parseShort(br.readLine());

  For byte:

  byte a=Byte.parseByte(br.readLine());

  For long:

  long a= Long.parseLong(br.readLine());

  For float:

  float a=Float.parseFloat(br.readLine());

  For double:

  double a=Double.parseDouble(br.readLine());

  For string:

  string s=br.readLine();

  For character:

  char ch=(char)br.read();

- **Take input using Scanner in various Data types:**

  Scanner sc=new Scanner(System.in);

  For interger:

  int a=sc.nextInt();

  For string:

  String s=sc.nextLine();

  For double:

  double a=sc.nextDouble();

  For float:

  float a=sc.nextFloat();

  For long:

  long a=sc.nextLong();

  For byte:

  byte a=sc.nextByte();

  For short:

  short a=sc.nextShort();

For Character:

char ch=sc.next().charAt(0);

Take input of a single word using Scanner:

String s=sc.next();

- **ASCII codes:**

65 to 90	A to Z
97 to 122	a to z
48 to 57	0 to 9
32	white space/space

QUESTIONS

Q1. Name the following:

(i) A package that is Invoked by default

(ii) A key word, to use the classes defined in a package.

Ans. (i) java.lang is the default package.

(ii) import is the keyword which is used to use the classes defined in a package.

For example: import java.util.Scanner;

Q2. Write the output of the following:

(i) System.out.println(Character.isUpperCase('R'));

(ii) System.out.println(Character.toUpperCase('J'));

Ans. (i) true

(ii) J

Q3. What are the two categories of packages?

Ans. (i) API (Application Programming Interface)

(ii) User defined packages.

Q4. What are Java API packages?

Ans. Java API has grouped large number of classes into many packages according to the functions performed by them. The classes of these packages can be imported to our program according to need.

Q5. Name the API package that contains wrapper classes.

Ans. java.lang

Q6. Which package needs to be imported whenever you accept the inputs from the keyboard using BufferedReader class.

Ans. java.io package

Q7. Name the wrapper class of (i) char (ii) long

Ans. (i) Character

(ii) Long

Q8. Write the output of the following:

(i) char ch = 'A';

int num = Character.toUpperCase(ch);

System.out.println(num);

Ans. 65

Q9. State the data type and value of res after the following code is executed:

char ch = 't';

res = Character.toUpperCase(ch);

Ans. data type of res should be **char**, and the value of res = 'T'

Q10. Give the output of the following code:

String A = "26", B = "100";

String D = A + B + "200";

int x = Integer.parseInt(A);

int y = Integer.parseInt(B);

int d = x + y;

System.out.println("Result 1 = " + D);

System.out.println("Result 2 = " + d);

Ans. Result 1 = 26100200

Result 2 = 126

PROGRAMS

P1. Write a program to enter a character through any input stream class. Check and print that the character is uppercase or lowercase.

P2. Write a program to enter a char value. If the value is an alphabet, print it in another case, i.e. if it is uppercase print it in lowercase and vice versa, otherwise print its ASCII code.

P3. Write a program to enter a char value. If it is an alphabet then print its next character (in the same case), otherwise print an appropriate message.

For example, if character is 'a' then print b.

2 ENCAPSULATION

1.1 Introduction: The basic goal of any abject oriented programming language is to provide mechanism that helps you to implement object oriented model. **Encapsulation** is an element of that mechanism.

Encapsulation binds code and data together and keep both safe from outside interference and misuse.

Wrapping up of data members and member functions into a single unit (class) is called encapsulation.

1.2 Access specifier/visibility modifiers: Encapsulation enables us to hide data. In java we implements encapsulation through the appropriate use of visibility modifiers.

Access specifiers help to restrict the scope of a class, constructor, variable, method or data member.

These are the following access modifiers available in java:

(i) Default: It is not a keyword. Here default means nothing. When no access modifier is specified, it is said to having the default access or friendly access of that member. The members having default access can be accessed in all classes within the same package.

(ii) Public: The public access modifier is specified using the keyword **public**. The public access modifier has the **widest scope** among all other access modifiers. They are accessible from everywhere in the program. There is no restriction on the scope of public member.

(iii) Private: The private access modifier is specified using keyword **private**. The methods or data members declared as private are accessible only **within the class** in which they are declared.

(iv) Protected: The protected access modifier is specified using the keyword **protected**. The methods or data members declared as protected are accessible **within the same package or subclasses in different packages**.

1.3 Scope and visibility rules: The term scope refers to the region where the variable can be accessed. Depending on the scope they are classified as instance variables, class variables and local variables. The following code helps to understand instance variable, class variable and local variable.

```
class Test
{
        int p;              // instance variable
        static int q;       // class variable
        void main()
        {
                int n;      // local variable
        }
}
```

- **Instance variables** are part of object of the class. They separately declared for every object of the class.
- **Class variables** are associated to the **class** rather than the object. They declared once for a class. After that their copy is shared among every object of the class. Class variables declared with **static** keyword.
- **Local variables** are associated to the function or section (like if, loop or switch) only in which they are declared.

1.4: Scope and visibility rules:

Visibility	Default	public	Protected	private
Same class	**Yes**	**Yes**	**Yes**	**Yes**
Class in same package	**Yes**	**Yes**	**Yes**	**No**
Subclass in same package	**Yes**	**Yes**	**Yes**	**No**
Subclass outside the same package	**No**	**Yes**	**Yes**	**No**
Non subclass outside the same package	**No**	**Yes**	**No**	**No**

1.5: Advantages of Encapsulation:

(i) Data hiding: We can hide data by using appropriate access specifiers and protects it from unwanted access by clients.

(ii) Flexibility: It allows access to a level without revealing the complex details below that levels.

(iii) Maintainability of the application is easy and improves.

SHORT ANSWER TYPE QUESTIONS

Q1. Name any two Oops principles.

Ans. (i) Encapsulation (ii) Inheritance

Q2. What does a class encapsulate?

Ans. Data (instance variables) and methods/functions.

Q3. Differentiate global and local variables.

Ans.

Global Variables	Local Variables
Global variables declared outside of the function body or in class body. They can be accessible in all methods of the class in which they are declared. Their scope may be instance variable or class variable.	Local variables declared in the method/block and confined to the method or block where they are declared.

Q4. Why is an object called an instance of a class?

Ans. Class encapsulates the data members and member functions. It is used to create an object as said. A class is an object factory. Hence, an object is called an instance of a class.

Q5. Why is a class known as composite data type?

Ans. Class is called a composite data type because it binds up (encapsulates) one or more primitive types together as a single data type.

For Example:

```
class Test
{
        int x;
        double y;
}
```

Q6. What is the difference between instance variables and class variables?

Ans.

Instance variables	Class variables
1. Instance variables are declared globally without **static** keyword.	1. Class variables are declared globally using **static** keyword.
2. Instance variables belong to object of the class. They declared separate for every object. Change the value in one class do not affect the other class.	2. Class variables belongs to class itself. There is only one copy of class variables shared between object of the class.

Q7. Which keyword is used to limit the accessibility of data?
Ans. private or protected.

Q8. What is the purpose of using the keyword final?

Ans. The **final** keyword is a non access specifier hat is used to restrict a class, variable and method. If we initialize a variable with final keyword, then we con not modify its value. If we declare a method as final, then it cannot be overridden by any subclasses.

3 STRING HANDLING

1.1 Introduction: We have discussed 8 **fundamental types**, which stores different numeric types, character and true and false values. Sometimes we need text (alphanumeric). In java **String** is a **reference type** of data which is used to store alpha numeric values.

String is a sequence of characters or group of characters. Unlike many other programming languages that implements string as Character array, java implements string as objects of type **String**. To work on string java provides a rich library of functions. For example, compare two strings, search for a substring and many more. Java **String** is **immutable** in nature, means once you created, you **cannot change** the characters that comprises it. You can still perform all types of operations. The difference is that each time you need an altered version of an existing string, a new string object is created that contains the modifications.

But if you want to change in the existing string then there is another companion class to **String** called **StringBuffer**.

Both the **String** and **StringBuffer** classes are defined in **java.lang**. Thus they are available to each program automatically. Both are declared final, which means that neither of these classes may be subclassed.

1.2 Using String class: **Strings** in java is used by declaring **String** type objects and initializing it with a string literal.

For example:

```
String str;                    // declaration of a String variable (object)
str = "Java is easy to learn"  // initialization of string variable
```

Internally java breaks String into **indexes**, which starts from **0**.

```
Hello Word
012345678910
```

Most functions work on these indexes. Space is also a character, so it has an index too.

1.3 Java class Methods:

Java operates on String using inbuilt library functions. Here is a list of some most used methods of java with their return type and example.

S. No.	Functions with their return type	Description	Example
1.	int length()	It returns the length or number of characters stored in a string variable (object) including spaces. Return type: **int**	String s = "Java is easy"; int len = s.length(); So value of len = 12 (Remember length() performs counting of characters so it does not start from index 0)
2.	char charAt(int)	It returns the character at index passed in the brackets. Return type: **char**	String s = "Java is easy"; char ch = s.charAt(2); so value of ch = v.

3.	int indexOf(char)	It returns the first occurrence (index) of the character passed in the brackets (if present). -1 returns otherwise.
		Return type: **int**
			String s = "Java is easy";
			int d = s.indexOf('a');
			int e = s.indexOf('p');
			so value of d = 1 and value of e = -1 as 'p' is not present in the string s.

4.	int lastIndexOf(char)	It returns the last occurrence (index) of the character passed in the brackets (if present). -1 returns otherwise.
		Return type: **int**
			String s = "Java is easy";
			int d = s.lastIndexOf('a');
			int e = s.lastIndexOf('p');
			so value of d = 9 and value of e = -1 as 'p' is not present in the string s.

5.	String trim()	It removes leading and trailing spaces. It does not remove spaces from middle of the string. Return type: **String**	String s = "Java is easy" String ns = s.trim(); So value of ns = Java is easy.
6.	String substring(int)	It returns part of the string from the value (index) passed in the brackets upto the end of string. Return type: **String**	String s = "Java is easy"; String ns = s.substring(2); So value of ns = va is easy
	String substring (int, int)	It returns part of the string from the first passing index to the second passing index (but excluding the second passing index). Return type: **String**	String s = "Java is easy"; String ns = s.substring(2, 10); So value of ns = va is ea

7.	boolean equals(String)	This function is used to compare two strings. It returns true if two strings are equal in terms of pattern and case, otherwise return false.
		Return type: **boolean**
			String s = "Java";
			String s1 = "java";
			String s2 = "java";
			String s3 = "Language";
			boolean b = s.equals(s1);
			boolean b1 = s.equals(s3);
			boolean b2 = s1.equals(s2);
			So values of b = false, b1 = false and b2 = true.

8.	boolean equalsIgnoreCase(String)	This function is used to compare two strings. It returns true if two strings are equal in terms of pattern, here case is not important, otherwise returns false.
		Return type: **boolean**
			String s = "Java";
			String s1 = "java";
			String s2 = "java";
			String s3 = "Language";
			boolean b = s.equalsIgnoreCase(s1);
			boolean b1 = s.equalsIgnoreCase(s3);

			boolean b2 = s1.equalsIgnoreCase(s2); So values of b = true, b1 = false and b2 = true.

9.	int compareTo(String)	This function compare two strings lexicographically (An art of writing Dictionary). It compares strings on the basis of their ASCII codes of first dissimilar character.
		Return type: **int**
		It returns –ve, 0 or +ve value.
		It is case sensitive.
			String s1 = "spade";
			String s2 = "space";
			String s3 = "special";
			String s4 = "Spade";
			int b1 = s1.compareTo(s2);
			int b2 = s1.compareTo(s3);
			int b3 = s1.compareTo(s4);
			So value of b1 = 1, b2 = -4 and b3 = 32

10.	int compareToIgnoreCase(String)	Same as compareTo, but it is not case sensitive.	String s1 = "Amit"; String s2 = "amit"; int b = s1.compareToIgnoreCase(s2); So value of b = 0
11.	String concat(String)	It is used to join or concatenate two strings one after another without any space. Return type: **String**	String s1 = "Java is"; String s2 = "easy to learn"; String s = s1.concat(s2); So value of s = Java iseasy to learn
12.	String replace(char oldChar,char newChar)	It replaces all old characters with new characters in a string, and returns it. Return type: **String**	String s1 = "Maryaram" String s = s1.replace('r', 'l'); So value of s = Malyalam

13.	boolean startsWith(String str)	It returns true if current string start with the string **str** as prefix otherwise false.
		Return type: **boolean**
		It is case sensitive.
			String s1 = "Butterfly flies";
			String str = "But";
			String s2 = "but";
			boolean b = s1.startsWith(str);
			boolean b1 = s1.startsWith(s2);
			So value of b = true and b1 = false

14.	boolean endsWith(String str)	It returns true if current string ends with the string **str** as suffix otherwise false.
		Return type: **boolean**
		It is case sensitive.
			String s1 = "Butterfly flies";
			String str = "ies";
			String s2 = "Ies";
			boolean b = s1.endsWith(str);
			boolean b1 = s1.endsWith(s2);
			So value of b = true and b1 = false

15.	String valueOf(all types)
	For example:
		It returns the String representation of the passed argument.
		Return type: **String**
			int n = 123;
			double d = 12.56;
			String s1 = String.valueOf(n);
			String s2 = String.valueOf(d);

	String valueOf(int) is used to change int to String and so on.		So value of s1 = 123 and s2 = 12.56 (these are in string form)

QUESTIONS

Q1: What is the difference(s) between **String** and **StringBuffer**?
Q2: What is the difference(s) between **length()** and **length**?
Q3: What is the difference(s) between **compareTo()** and **equals()**? Give an example of each..
Q4: What is the difference(s) between 'a' and "a" ?
Q5: Define use of static in variable declaration.
Q6: Write a valid java statement to initializes 5 names in a string array
Q7: Write a statement for each to perform the following task on a String:
(i) Extract the third character of a word stored in the variable str.
(ii) Check if the second character of a string is in lowercase.
Q8: What is the difference between isUpperCase() and toUpperCase() functions ?
Q9: Write the return type of the following functions: **[Boards 2019]**
(i) startWith( )
(ii) random( )

PROGRAMS

P1: Write a program to enter a String and print its length.
P2: Write a program to enter a string and print each of its character in new line.
P3: Write a program to enter a string and print it in reverse order.
Input : This is a cat
Output:

- sihT si a tac
- cat a is This
- tac a si sihT

P4: Write a program to enter a string and perform all library functions on it.
P5: Write a program to enter a string and store its reverse string in a string variable and then print that variable.
P6: Write a program to enter a word and check is it palindrome or not. Example of palindrome words are MADAM, NITIN, ARORA etc.
P7: Write a program to enter a string and count no of vowels present in the string, then print the frequency of all vowels presents in the string (ignore the case).
Input : I am good in java.
Output : Frequency of Vowels : 7
P8: Write a program to enter a string and count no of vowels present in the string, then print the frequency of all vowels separately (each in a new line).
P9: Write a program of pig latin:
Example: king=> ingkay, LONDON => ONDONLAY etc.
P10: Write a program to enter a string and encrypt it as
India=> Kpfkc (replace each character by its second character)

P11: Write a program to enter a string (assume in upper case) and print frequency of all characters present in the string.

P12: Write a program to enter a name and print it as

Input: Sachin Ramesh Tendulkar

Output: S.R.Tendulkar or Tendulkar S R

P13: Write a program to replace a character with a given character in a string (don't use replace fuction).

Input : Matter

Output : Manner (Replaced 'n' with 't').

P14: Write a program to replace a word with a given word.

Input : the book is on the table (replace 'the' with 'that'

Output : that book is on that table.

P15: Write a program to count no of words in a given string. (Leading and trailing spaces are not counted and between two words only one space is allowed.

Input : Java   is   easy   to learn.

Output : Total words = 5

P16: Write a program to enter some text and print all consecutive characters from it.

Example: Input string : UNDERSTAND

Output: DE RS ST

P17: Input a sentence in any random case and capitalize the first and last letter of each word and convert the rest to lower case.

Input : Love all Hate none.

Output : LovE AlL HatE NonE.

P18: Write a program to accept a string and display the number of upper case characters, number of lowercase characters and number of digits present in the string.

Input : Common Wealth Games 2010

Output : No. of upper case characters : 3

No. of lower case characters : 14

No. of digits : 4

P19: Write a program to input a name. Convert each letter to its opposite case. Print the original and modified name along with suitable messages.

Input : Rahul Dravid

Output :

Original name: Rahul Dravid

Modified name: rAHUL dRAVID

P20: Write a program to input a sentence. Print the longest and the smallest word from the sentence along with its length.

Input : Honesty is the best policy.

Output : Longest word : Honesty (length = 7)

Smallest word : is (length = 2)

P21: Input a word and generate the following pattern

Input: MATHS

Output:

(i)		(ii)		(iii)		(iv)	
	M		MATHS		MATHS		MATHS
	MA		MATH		MATH		ATHS
	MAT		MAT		MAT		THS
	MATH		MA		MA		HS
	MATHS		M		M		S

P22: Write a menu driven program to display the pattern as per user's choice . **[Boards 2018]**

Pattern 1	Pattern 2
ABCDE	B
ABCD	LL
ABC	UUU
AB	EEEE
A	

P23: Write a program to create a function arrange(String s), such that it first convert the word into capital. Arrange each letter of the word in alphabetical order. Print the word before and after arranging letters in A-Z order.

Example: Input: India

Output:

Given word : India

Word in capitals : India

Word after sorting : ADIIN

P24: Write a program in java to accept a string in lower case and change the first letter of every word to upper case. Display the new string. **[Boards 2018]**

Sample input : we are in the cyber world.

Sample output : We Are In The Cyber World

P25: Design a class to overload a function check ( ) as follows: **[Boards 2017]**

(i) void check (String str, char ch): to find and print the frequency of the character in a string.

Example:

Input	Output
str = "success"	number of 's' present is = 3
ch = 's'	

(ii) void check (String s1): to display only vowels from string s1, after converting it to lower case.

Example:

Input	Output
s1 = "Computer"	o u e

P26: Write a program to enter a sentence and convert it into uppercase and count and display the total number of words starting with a letter 'A'. **[Boards 2019]**

Sample Input: ADVANCEMENT AND APPLICATION OF INFORMATION TECHNOLOGY ARE EVER CHANGING.

Sample Output: Total number of words starting with letter 'A' = 4.

OUTPUT

O1: Give the output of the flowing statements:

```
System.out.print("India".toUpperCase());
System.out.print("Mohit".equals("mohit"));
System.out.print("MUMBAI".charAt(2));
System.out.print("Mumbai.indexOf('m'));
```

O2: What is print by the following code.

```
String str="Application";
System.out.println(str.charAt(str.indexOf('p')));
System.out.println(str.indexOf(str.charAt(2)));
```

03: On the basis of the following array of string answer the given questions:

String str[ ]={"Singapore","Mumbai","Delhi","Banglore"};

What is range of the indices of the array str.

System.out.println(str[3].length());

System.out.println(str.length);

04: Give Output of the following statements:

```
String s1="Computer";
String s2="COMPUTER";
String s3="intel";
String s4="ICSE";
System.out.println(s1.equals(s2));
System.out.println(s1.compareTo(s2));
System.out.println(s1.compareToIgnoreCase(s2));
System.out.println(s1.compareToIgnoreCase(s3));
System.out.println(s2.equals(s1.toUpperCase()));
System.out.println(s1.indexOf('a'));
System.out.println(s3 + s1);
System.out.println(s3 + s2.substring(1,5));
System.out.println(s1.substring(3));
System.out.println(s2.charAt(s4.indexOf('E')));
System.out.println(s1.substring(s4.length(),s3.length()));
```

05: State the output when the following program segment is executed.

```
String a="SmartPhone" b="Graphic Art";
String h=a.substring(2,5);
String k=b.substring(8).toUpperCase();
System.out.println(h);
System.out.println(k.equalsIgnoreCase(h));
```

06: Write the output of the following: **[Boards 2019]**

```
String s1 = "Phoenix"; String s2 = "island";
System.out.println(s1.substring((0).concat(s2.substring(2)));
System.out.println(s2.toUpperCase());
```

ARRAYS (SUBSCRIPTED VARIABLE)

1.1 Introduction: To make a program we need values and to store them we need variables/data. It is okay to work with a limited number of variables, but to work with programs like 'store age of 50 students in a class', is a tedious task because one cannot remember 50 variables. Code will take space too. So to avoid this complexity we create **set** of **similar type** of variables called **Array**. It is not a keyword.

1.2 Array: Array is a collection of similar types of values with the same name. An array stores on **continuous** memory locations. Internally it is divided into **indexes/subscript**. Indexes in Array starts from 0. Every index represents one value. Array is a reference type of data.

Types of array: Depending upon the structure , Array is divided into the following parts:
(i) Single Dimensional Array (SDA) or One Dimensional Array.
(ii) Double Dimensional Array (DDA) or Two Dimensional Array.

1.3 Understanding Single Dimensional Array: Single dimensional array can be treated as a set of elements in a row or in a coloumn.

- **Syntax of declaration of an array:** <data type> <array name>[ ] = new <data type>[size]

For example **int arr[ ] = new int [5]** will create an array of 5 elements, which can stores 5 different data values. It is equivalent to taking five variables with five different names. Index of array starts from 0. Statement **int arr[ ] = new int [5]** is same as statement **int [ ]arr = new int [5]**. This statement creates 5 variables of same name as **arr[0], arr[1], arr[2], arr[3]** and **arr[4]**. In memory it will looks like following:

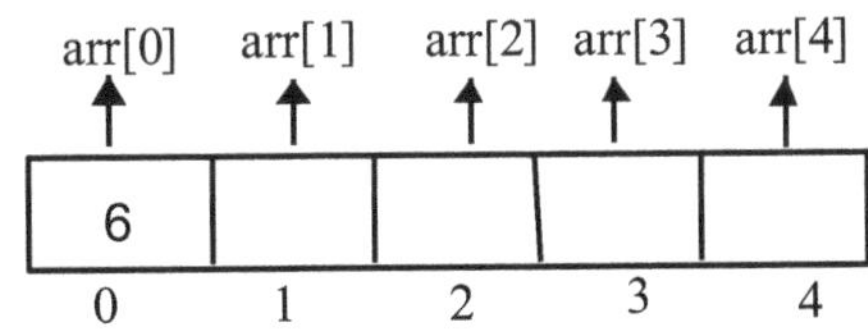

and **arr[0] = 6** will store 6 at 0 index. We can take input through **Scanner** class as well.
For Example: arr[1] = sc.nextInt( ) // sc is an object of class Scanner.

- **Initialization of Single Dimensional array:** int [ ] = {2, 3, 5, 7, 11}. This statement will declare and initialize an array with first five prime numbers.

PROGRAM

Write a program to enter 10 elements in single dimensional array. Print all even numbers from the array.

Solution:

```
import java.util.*;
class Even
{
    Public static void main(String args[ ])
    {
        Scanner sc = new Scanner(System.in);
```

```
                int arr[ ]= new int[10], i;                          // declaration of array
                for (i = 0 ; i < 10 ; i++)                      // start a loop from 0 to n – 1 for index
                {
                        System.out.println("Enter value ");
                        arr[i] = sc.nextInt();                  // stores value through keyboard one by one.
                }
                for (i = 0 ; i < 10 ; i ++)
                {
                        if(arr[i] % 2 == 0)
                                System.out.println(arr[i]);
                }
        }
}
```

1.4 Finding length or number of elements in an array: If we need to find the number of elements in an array. A property **length** is used, which return the size of the associated array.

For Example:

```
class Test
{
        public static void main(String args[ ])
        {
                int arr[ ]= {2, 4, 6, 8, 9};
                int len = arr.length;
                System.out.println("Number of elements in the Array = " + len);
        }
}
```

Output: Number of elements in the Array = 5

Remark: Do not confuse with **length (property** to find length of an array) with **length( ),** which is a **function**, to find length of a **String.**

1.5 Searching and Sorting in Single Dimensional Array:

Searching: The process of finding an element in an array is called searching. There are two searching techniques used depending on sorted or unsorted array:

1. Linear Search Technique
2. Binary Search Technique

1. Linear Search Technique: It is also termed as Sequential Search. This technique search desired element in the array sequentially i.e. from the 0th index one by one. It can be applied on both types of array sorted or unsorted.

Program: Write a program to enter an element from a given array using Linear Search Technique. Print appropriate message.

```
class Linear
{
        public static void main(int arr[ ],int n)
        {
                int f=0,i;
                int l=arr.length;
                for(i=0;i<l;i++)
                {
```

```
                if(arr[i]==n)
                {
                        f=1;
                        break;
                }
        }
        if(f==1)
                System.out.println("search successful");
        else
                System.out.println("search not successful");
    }
}
```

1. Binary Search Technique: This method follows the divide and conquers approach in which the array is divided into two halves repeatedly until all elements examine. It can be applied on sorted array only. It is faster than the linear search.

Program: Write a program to enter an element from a given sorted array (in ascending order) using Binary Search Technique. Print appropriate message.

```
import java.util.*;
class Binary
{
        public static void main(int arr[])
        {
                Scanner sc=new Scanner(System.in);
                int i,j,temp,l;
                l=arr.length;
                System.out.println("enter a no to search");
                int n=sc.nextInt();
                int low=0,high=l-1,mid,f=0;
                while(low<=high)
                {
                        mid=(low+high)/2;
                        if(arr[mid]==n)
                        {
                                f=1;
                                break;
                        }
                        else if(n>arr[mid])
                                low=mid+1;
                        else
                                high=mid-1;
                }
                if(f==1)
                        System.out.println("no is found");
                else
                        System.out.println("no is not found");
        }
}
```

QUESTIONS

Q1: What is an array?

Q2: What is the following statement doing
int arr[ ]=new int[5];

Q3: How many bytes will be reserved for the following statements?
int arr[]=new int[6];
int arr[][]=new int[4][3];

Q4: Write a statement in java to initializes a character array with the following characters:
*, /, M, ~, ! , | (comma is used for separation)

Q5: Write a Java statement to initializes an integer array with following numbers
3, 7, 21, 156, 31

Q6: What is the pre-requisite of Binary Search?

Q7: Given an integer array arr[ ]={3,1,5,6,7,2}
Answer the following
(i) What is the value of arr.length?
(ii) What is the value of arr[4]?
(iii) What is the first and last index of arr[ ]?

Q8: What is the difference between searching and sorting?

Q9: What is the difference between Linear & Binary search techniques?

Q10: Write a statement to print the last element of an array arr[]

Q11: List the variables from those given below that are composite type.

(i)	static int x;	(iv)	boolean b;
(ii)	arr[i] = 10;	(v)	private char chr;
(iii)	obj.display( );	(vi)	String str;

PROGRAMS

P1: Write a program to input 10 integers in an array and print them in reverse order.

P2: Write a program to input 'n' integers in an array and print the sum of all the integers entered by the user. Also print the average of elements.

P3: Write a program to input a number 'n' and input 'n' numbers in an array. Now print all those numbers which are greater than 10.

P4: Write a program to input 10 integers and input a searching element 'n'. Now search for 'n' in the array using linear search technique. If n exists print the position of n else print an appropriate message.

P5: Write a program to input 'n' elements in an array and print the largest and the smallest number of the array. Also print their positions.

P6: Write a program to input two arrays arr1 and arr2 each of size 5. Now store the sum of two arrays in a third array arr3. E.g Input - arr1 – 5,1,2,5,3 arr2 – 8,5,0,1,4 Output-13, 6, 2, 6, 7

P7: Write a program to input two array arr1 and arr2 of size 'm' and 'n' respectively (m and n to be entered by the user). Now merge two arrays in arr3 as shown in the example.
E.g. Input – m=5, n=4, arr1 – 4,1,8,7,5 arr2 – 2,7,1,9 Output arr3- 4,1,8,7,5,2,7,1,9

P8: Write a program to print all prime numbers from an array of 10 elements.

P9: Write a program to create a single dimensional array of n integers (n is entered by user). Print only those elements from the array which are Armstrong.

P10: Write a function **void print()** which accept an array of 20 integers and print the sum of all the integers which are present at odd addresses.

P11: Write a program to enter 10 names and their phone numbers in two different arrays. Ask user to enter a name and print corresponding phone number if present along with name (use linear search technique).

P12: Write a program to take input n (even) elements in an array. Print GCD/HCF of every two sets of integers.

For example: let arr[ ] = {4, 24, 9, 15, 36, 75}, GCD of (4, 24), (9, 15) and (36, 75) should be printed.

P13: Write a function **void search(int arr[], int n)** which search the element 'n' in the array using binary search method (array should be in arranged in ascending order).

P14: Two single dimensional arrays contain the elements as follows:

X[ ]={5,-3,-2,1,0,12,14,16,25,13}

Y[ ]={6,5,10,15,18,20,22,30}

Write a program that results a third array z as follows:

Z[ ]={5,6,-3,5,-2,10,1,15,0,18,12,20,14,22,16,30,25,13}

P15: Write a program to input and store roll numbers, names and marks in 3 subjects of n number of students in five single dimensional array and display the remark based on the average marks as given below (The maximum marks in the subject are 100).

$$\text{Average marks} = \frac{\text{total marks}}{3}$$ (Average should be round off to the nearest integer)

Average marks	Remarks
85-100	Excellent
75-84	Distinction
60-74	First Class
40-59	Pass
Less than 40	Poor

P16: Write a program to accept name and total marks of N number of students in two single subscript arrays **name**[ ] and **totalmarks**[ ].

Calculate and print:

(i) The average of the total marks obtained by N number of students.
[average = (sum of total marks of all the students)/N]

(ii) Deviation of each student's total marks with the average.
[deviation = total marks of a student - average]

OUTPUT

O1: What will this code print.

```
int arr[]=new int[5];
System.out.print(arr);
```

(i) 0 (ii) value stored in arr[0] (iii) Error (iv) Garbage value

O2: String x[ ]= {"Artificial intelligence", "IOT", "Machine learning", "Big data"} **[Boards 2019]**

Give the output of the following statements:

(i) System.out.println(x[3]);

(ii) System.out.println(x.length);

03: Consider the following String array and give the output:

```
String arr[ ] = {"DELHI", "CHENNAI", "MUMBAI", "LUCKNOW", "JAIPUR"};
System.out.println(arr[0].length( ) > arr[3].length());
System.out.println(arr[4].substring(0, 3));
System.out.println(arr.length);
```

5 EXCEPTION HANDLING

1.1 Introduction: The exception handling is a mechanism of java which allows user to control the **unexpected** termination of the application due to some unexpected situations during the compilation/execution of the program. Situations like **divide by zero**, **number format mismatch** etc. may terminate the smooth functioning of the program. Java provides **try** and **catch** block to handle these types of situations and many more.

Exception: It is an unexpected situation which arises as run time error in the java program. To overcome with these types of errors is known as exception handling. This is done using some pre defined constraints like **try, catch** etc.

Example of some exceptions are:

(i) NumberFormatException	It appears when an invalid number format encountered
(ii) ArrayIndexOutOfBoundException	It appears when array index is not within the range.
(iii) IOException	Appears due to some input/output problems.

Error: The errors in a program appear due to various reasons like mistake in typing the program, misspelling, incorrect logic etc. Errors can be of three types.

- Compile time error
- Run time error
- Logical error

QUESTIONS

Q1: Define exception. Name some exception.
Q2: Define exception handling and state any two advantages of exception handling.
Q3: What is the need of **try** and **catch** block in exception handling?
Q4: What do you mean by keyword **throws**?
Q5: State the difference between **throw** and **throws**
Q6: Name the block that always get executed no matter which kind of exception is thrown.
Q7: What is the use of **finally()** block in exception handling?
Q8: What is the difference between **final** and **finally**?
Q9: Where does catch appear in the program?
Q10. Explain compile time error and run time error.

6 OUTPUT QUESTIONS

ARRAYS

Q1: What is wrong in the following code? Explain. Also write correct form of the following-

```
int u; [ ] = new int[6];
u = {2, 5, 6, 7, 8, 9};
```

Q2: Is any of the following is incorrect? Explain.

```
(i) int y[ ] = new int[100];
(ii) int [ ]d = new int[100];
```

Q3: Given that : int b[ ] = {2, 66, 76, 23, 78, 96};
Give the subscripts (indexes) of 76 and 78.

Q4: What will be the output of the following code?

```
int  x[ ] = {4, 8, 2, 6 };
int  y[ ] = {6, 9, 4, 8 };
x = y;
System.out.print("\n x[2]=" + x[2]);
System.out.print("\n y[2]=" + y[2]);
```

Q5: What will be output of the following code?

```
int [ ] ar = {2, 5, 8, 9, 1, 6, 4, 3, 5 };
System.out.println(ar.length);
```

Q6: What will be the output of the following code?

```
int ar [ ] = {2, 5, 8, 9, 1, 6, 4, 9, 3, 5 };
System.out.println(ar [3+4]);
System.out.println(ar[1+3]);
System.out.println(ar[5-3]);
```

Q7: Find the errors and correct them (if any): int ar( ) = {2, 5, 7, 9, 4, 6 };

Q8: Given that d[ ] = {4, 6, 5, 7, 8, 9}

```
for(int i = 0 ; i < d.length – 1 ; i ++)
System.out.print(d[i] + d[i + 1])
```

Q9: What will be the ouput of the following code?

```
int ar [ ] ={2, 5, 8, 9, 1, 6, 4, 9, 3, 5};
System.out.println(ar [3] * 2);
System.out.println(ar[4] + 3);
System.out.println(ar[6+2] * 3);
```

Q10: Answer the following questions:

int ar [ ] ={2, 5, 8, 9, 1, 6, 4, 9, 3, 5 };

(i) State the start and end indices of ar[ ].

(ii) State the element stored at 3rd and 7th index.

(iii) State whether sum of elements from 0 to 4 indexes are more than sum of elements from 5 to 9 indexes or not.

Q11: Write Java statements to perform the following-

(i) to declare a single subscripted variable of 20 integers.

(ii) to declare single subscripted variable of 14 real numbers.

(iii) to initialize first 10 even numbers in a single dimensional array.

Q12: Give the output of the following function when invoked?

```
void show( )
{
        int y[ ] = {2, 4, 5, 8};
        int q = y.length; int p = 0;
        for(int j = 0; j < q; j++).
        {
                p=y[j] + y[3 – j];
                System.out.println (p);
        }
}
```

Q13: Give the output of the following code:

```
int ar [ ] = {3, 4, 5, 6};
for(int j = 0; j<4; j++)
{
        for(int n = 0; n<=j; n++)
        {
                System.out.println(ar[n]+ " ");
        }
        System.out.println("\n");
}
```

Q14: Give the output of the following code:

```
int z [ ] = {39, 42, 36, 45, 75, 98 };
System.out.print(z[3] + "," + z[4]*2
```

LIBRARY CLASSES (String Handling)

Q1: Give output of following statements:

(i) System.out.println("Lucknow".toUpperCase( ));

(ii) System.out.println("England".charAt(4));

(iii) System.out.println("Nice".equals("nice"));

(iv) String st = "this is final examination";
System.out.println(st.length( ));

Q2: Give output for following java statements if a =2, b = 3 initially:

(i) System.out.println(a + (+ + b));

(ii) System.out.println("S".toLowerCase( ));

(iii) System.out.println("India".compareTo("country"));

(iv) System.out.println(Math.pow(a, b));

Q3: What will be output of the following statements?

String a = "Computer";

String b = "Applications";

(i) System.out.println(a + b);

(ii) System.out.println(a.substring(3));

(iii) System.out.println(a.equals(b));

(iv) System.out.println(a.charAt(2));

Q4: Write valid java statements to perform the following tasks on strings:

(i) Extract first 10 characters from a string object str.

(ii) To print the position of the first occurrence of the letter 'B' in the string object str.

(iii) Print the length of the string stored in object str.

(iv) Convert the string stored in str in uppercase form.

Q5: Give output of the following:

(i) System.out.println("ComPUter".toUpperCase( ));

(ii) System.out.println("ProGRam".charAt(4));

(iii) String ss= "My Book";
System.out.println(ss.length( ));

(iv) System.out.println("great".indexOf('e'));

(v) System.out.println("great".equalsIgnoreCase ("GREAT'));

(vi) String ss= "Good".concat("Bye");
System.out.println(ss);

Q6: Give output of the following Java code:

```
String str = "COMPUTER";
char ch = str.charAt( 9/2 );
int as = ch;
System.out.println(as + "\t" + (char)( as ));
```

Q7: Given output of following program code if method is invoked as test("XYZ");

```
void test( String n)
 {
        String  st = n + "ABC";
```

```
        System.out.println( "n =" + n );
        System.out.println( "st=" + st );
}
```

Q8: Write a valid Java statement to assign 8 names of countries in the string array.

Q9: What is the output of the following code:

```
String x = "hello";
String y = "world";
(i)     System.out.println( x + y );
(ii)    System.out.println(x.length( ));
(iii)   System.out.println( x.charAt(3));
(iv)    System.out.println( x.equals(y ));
```

Q10: Consider the following program code. Underline the errors and rewrite the correct program code:

```
Public Class test
{
        public static void main( String args[ ] )
        {
        String  ns = "10th std";
        System.out.println("I am class X student");
        System.out.println("I am studying in" ns + "\t");
        System.out.println("This is the output");
        }
}
```

Q11: Write a statement to declare and initialize a character array of five capital vowels.

Q12: Give the output for following program code:

```
String sat = "ExAmInATioN";
for(int y = 0; y<sat.length( ); y+=2)
{
        System.out.print ( sat.char At( y ) + " ");
}
```

Q13: Give output of the following program code:

```
String text = "APPLICATION";
for(int k = text.length( )-1;  k>=0; k- -)
{
        for( int y=0; y<=k; y + +)
        {
            System.out.print( text.charAt( y ));
        }
        System.out.print("\n");
}
```

Q14: Give the output of the following code:

```
String A = "26", B = "100";
String D = A + B + "200";
int x = Integer.parseInt (A);
```

```
int y = Integer.parseInt (B);
int d = x + y + 200;
System.out.print ("Result 1 =" + D);
System.out.print ("Result 2 =" +d);
```

Q15: Give the output of the following code:

```
long x = 30, y = 40;
Sring A, B;  String  S;
A = String.valueOf (x);
B = String.valueOf (y);
System.out.println("Output 1 =" + x + y);
System.out.println("Output 2 =" +A + B);
S = A + B;
System.out.println("Output 3 =" + (x + y));
System.out.print("Output 4 =" + S);
```

Q16: Give the output of the folloiwng code:

```
System.out.println("Finder".endsWith("der"));
System.out.println("Better".startsWith("Bet"));
```

Q17: Write a statement to cheak if the second character of a string str is in uppercae ?

Solved Question Papers

Practice Paper – 1 (Solved)

Computer Application

(Time allotted: One and a half hour)

Maximum Marks: 50

Attempt all questions from **section A** and any four questions from **section B.**

The intended marks for questions or part of questions are given in the brackets [ ].

Section A (10 Marks)

(Attempt all questions from this section)

Question1:

Choose the correct answer to the questions from the given options. (Do not write the question, write the correct answer only.) **[10]**

(i) Which is the default java package:

(a) java.lang

(b) java.util

(c) java.awt

(d) java.io

Solution: Correct option is (a)

(i) Which one is not a keyword in java?

(a) break

(b) default

(c) int

(d) true

Solution: Correct option is (d)

(iii) What will be the output of the following code?

int ar [ ] = {2, 5, 8, 9, 1, 6, 4, 9, 3, 5 };

system.out.println(ar [3+4]};

(a) 6

(b) 7

(c) 9

(d) 5

Solution: Correct option is (c)

(iv) Act of combining of data and its associated functions into a single unit is known as ________

(a) Polymorphism

(b) Encapsulation

(c Inheritance

(d) Data abstraction

Solution: Correct option is (b)

(v) Which visibility modifier gives the least access?

(a) Public

(b) Private

(c) Protected

(d) None

Solution: Correct option is (b)

(vi) What will be output of the following statement?

String a = "Computer";
String b = "Applications".
System.out.println(a.compareTo(b));

(a) true

(b) false

(c) 2

(d) −2

Solution: correct option is (c)

(vii) System.out.println(" ProGRam".charAt(4));

(a) r

(b) G

(c) R

(d) A

Solution: Correct option is (c)

(viii) A variable that is bounded to the object itself is called:

(a) Instance

(b) class

(c) Argument

(d) local

Solution: Correct option is (a)

(ix) Write the correct output of the following code:

String str = "This is a cat".
System.out.println(str.indexOf(str.charAt(11));

(a) a

(b) 11

(c) 8

(d) T

Solution: Correct option is (c)

(x) If, arr[ ] = {2, 4, 7, 9, 3};
what is arr[2]

(a) 4

(b) 2

(c) 9

(d) 7

Solution: Correct option is (d)

Section B (40 Marks)
(Attempt any four questions from this section)

Question 2: **[10]**

Write a program to enter a string and print it in reverse order.
Input: This is a cat
Output: sihT si a tac

Solution:

```
import java.util.*;
class Reverse
{
	public static void main(String args[ ])
	{
		Scanner sc = new Scanner(System.in);
		String str, w = "";
		int i,len;
		System.out.println("Enter a string");
		str = sc.nextLine( );
		str = str + "  ";			//concate a space at the end of the string
		len = str.length( );			//storing length of the string in len
		for(i = 0 ; i < len ; i++)
		{
			char ch = str.charAt(i);
			if(ch == ' ')			//if ch contains a space
			{
				System.out.print(w + " ");
				w = "";			//emptying string after printing
			}
			else
				w = ch + w;		//forming a reverse word
		}
	}
}
```

Question 3: **[10]**

Write a program to input 'n' elements in an array and print the largest and the smallest number of the array. Also print their Difference.

Solution:

```
import java.util.*;
class LargeSmall
```

```
{
        public static void main (String args[ ])
        {
                Scanner sc = new Scanner (System.in);
                int arr[ ],n,i;                                  //declaration of array and variables
                System.out.println("Enter the limit for an array");
                n = sc.nextInt();
                arr=new int[n];
                System.out.println("Enter elements in an array");
                for (i=0 ; i<n ; i++)                            //input in array
                {
                        System.out.println("Enter elements");
                        arr[i]=sc.nextInt();
                }
                int sml=arr[0];
                int lar=arr[0];
                for(i=0 ; i<n ; i++)                             //finding largest and smallest elements
                {
                if(arr[i]>lar)
                        lar=arr[i];
                if(arr[i]<sml)
                        sml=arr[i];
        }
        System.out.println("Largest element is "+lar);
        System.out.println("Smallest element is "+sml);
        System.out.println("Difference = "+(lar - sml));
    }
}
```

Question 4: **[10]**

Write a program in java to accept a string in lower case and print all consecutive double characters.
Sample Input: I am f<u>ee</u>ding an a<u>pp</u>le to a ra<u>bb</u>it
Sample Output: 3

Solution:

```
import java.util.*;
class Rabbit
{
public static void main(String args[ ])
{
        Scanner sc = new Scanner(System.in);
        String str;
        int i, count = 0, len;
        System.out.println("Enter a string");
        str = sc.nextLine();
        len = str.length();                              //finding length of the string
        str = str.toLowerCase( );                        //converting string into lower case
```

```
        for(i = 0 ; i < len - 1 ; i++)
        {
                char ch = str.charAt(i);
                char ch1 = str.charAt(i + 1);
                if(ch == ch1)                          //comparison of characters
                        count++;
        }
        System.out.println(count);
    }
}
```

Question 5: **[10]**

Write a code in java to enter two arrays. One containing names of country and other containing their corresponding capitals. Ask user to input a country name and search that name in the array using BINARY SEARCH technique. If the name of that country is found then print its corresponding capital otherwise print appropriate message.

[Assume that both arrays are arranged according to country array in A to Z format]

Solution:

```
import java.util.*;
class Country
{
        public static void main(String cn[ ], String cp[ ])
        {
                Scanner sc = new Scanner(System.in);
                int i, l, low = 0, high,flag = 0,mid = 0;
                l = cn.length;                              //finding length of the string
                high = l - 1;
                System.out.println("Enter a Country name to search");
                String str = sc.nextLine();
                while(low <= high)
                {
                        mid = (low + high)/2;               //finding mid index of the string

                        if(str.compareToIgnoreCase(cn[mid]) == 0)
                        {
                                flag = 1;
                                break;
                        }
                        else if (str.compareToIgnoreCase(cn[mid]) > 0)
                                low = mid + 1;
                        else
                                high = mid - 1;
                }
                if(flag == 1)
                        System.out.println(cp[mid]);
                else
                        System.out.println("Country not found");
```

```
        }
}
```

Question 6: **[10]**

Write a program to input two arrays arr1 and arr2 each of size 5. Now store the sum of two arrays in a third array arr3. E.g Input - arr1 – 5,1,2,5,3 arr2 – 8,5,0,1,4 Output-13, 6, 2, 6, 7

Solution:

```
import java.util.*;
class AddArray
{
        public static void main(String args[ ])
        {
                Scanner sc = new Scanner(System.in);
                int arr1[]=new int[5],arr2[]=new int[5],sum[]=new int[5];
                                                        //declaration of three arrays
                int i;
                System.out.println("Enter elements in the first array");
                for(i=0 ; i<5 ; i++)
                        arr1[i]=sc.nextInt();
                System.out.println("Enter elements in the second array");
                for(i=0 ; i<5 ; i++)
                        arr2[i]=sc.nextInt();
                for(i=0 ; i<5 ; i++)                        //addition of both arrays
                        sum[i]=arr1[i]+arr2[i];
                System.out.println("Printing of the sum of both arrays\n");
                        for(i=0 ; i<5 ; i++)                //printing of final array
                System.out.println(sum[i]);
        }
}
```

Question 7: **[10]**

Write a program to enter a word and check is it palindrome or not.
Example of palindrome words are MADAM, NITIN, ARORA etc.

Solution:

```
import java.util.*;
class Palindrome
{
        public static void main(String args[ ])
        {
                Scanner sc = new Scanner(System.in);
                String str,rev="";
                int i, count = 0, len;
                System.out.println("Enter a string");
                str = sc.nextLine();                //inputting of a word
                len = str.length();                 //finding length
                str = str.toUpperCase( );           //converting into upper case
```

```
		for(i = 0 ; i < len ; i++)
		{
			char ch = str.charAt(i);
			rev = ch + rev;				//reversing the word
		}
		if(rev.equals(str))
			System.out.println("Palindrome");
		else
			System.out.println("Not Palindrome");
	}
}
```

Practice Paper – 2 (Solved)

Computer Application

(Time allotted: One and a half hour)

Maximum Marks: 50

Attempt all questions from **section A** and any four questions from **section B.**

The intended marks for questions or part of questions are given in the brackets [ ].

Section A (10 Marks)

(Attempt all question from this section)

Question1:

Choose the correct answer to the questions from the given options. (Do not write the question, write the correct answer only.) **[10]**

(i) The access modifier that gives most access:

(a) package
(b) private
(c) protected
(d) public

Solution: Correct option is (d)

(ii) According to java naming convention which is invalid:

(a) fnc( )
(b) fnc123( )
(c) 123fnc( )
(d) Fnc( )

Solution: Correct option is (c)

(iii) which keyword is used to inform that an error has encountered?

(a) throws
(b) try
(c) break
(d) catch

Solution: Correct option is (a)

(iv) int res = 'a'
What is the value of res?

(a) 65
(b) 97
(c) a
(d) None

Solution: Correct option is (b)

(v) What is the return type of the function compareTo( )?

(a) boolean
(b) long
(c) String
(d) int

Solution: Correct option is (d)

(vi) Which function is used to compare two strings lexicographically?

(a) equals( )
(b) compareTo( )
(c) max( )
(d) equallexico( )

Solution: Correct option is (b)

(vii) What will be the output of the following code?

```
int  x[ ] = {4, 8, 2, 6 };
int  y[ ] = {6, 9, 4, 8 };
system.out.print(x[2] + y[3]);
```

(a) 10
(b) 5
(c) 12
(d) 28

Solution: Correct option is (a)

(viii) classes are grouped together to make a:

(a) function
(b) array
(c) package
(d) None

Solution: Correct option is (c)

(ix) How many bytes are consumed by the following array in memory?

```
int arr[ ] = new int[10];
```

(a) 10 bytes
(b) 20 bytes
(c) 40 bytes
(d) 80 bytes

Solution: Correct option is (c)

(x) long x = 30, y = 40;

```
String A, B;
A = String.valueOf (x);
```

```
B = String.valueOf (y);
System.out.println(A + B);
```

(a) 70

(b) 3040

(c) 1200

(d) 4030

Solution: Correct option is (b)

Section B (40 Marks)
(Attempt any Four questions from this section)

Question 2: **[10]**

Write a program to input integer elements into an array of size 20 and perform the following operations:
(i) Display sum of all elements of the array.
(ii) Find the average of elements of the array.

Solution:

```
import java.util.*;
class Largest
{
        public static void main(String args[])
        {
                Scanner sc = new Scanner(System.in);
                int arr[ ] = new int[20], i, sum = 0;
                double avg;
                System.out.println("Enter numbers in the array");
                for(i = 0 ; i < 20 ; i++)                    //Input numbers in array
                {
                        arr[i] = sc.nextInt( );
                }
                for(i = 0 ; i < 20 ; i++)
                {
                        sum = sum + arr[i];
                }
                avg = (double)sum / 20;                      //typecasting int into double
                System.out.println("Sum of elements is " + sum);
                System.out.println("Average of elements is " + avg);
        }
}
```

Question 3: **[10]**

Write a program to enter a string. Print all words from the string which start with vowels.
Sample Input :Amrita is very intelligent student
Sample Output: Amrita is intelligent

Solution:

```
import java.util.*;
class Vowels
{
        public static void main(String args[ ])
        {
                Scanner sc = new Scanner(System.in);
                String v = "AEIOUaeiou", str, w = "";
                int i, len;
                System.out.println("Enter a sentence"");
                str = sc.nextLine( );
                str = str + " ";                        //adding a space to the last of string
                len = str.length( );                    //finding length of the string
                for(i = 0 ; i < len ; i ++)
                {
                        char ch = str.charAt(i);
                        if(ch == ' ')
                        {
                                if(v.indexOf(w.charAt(0)) >= 0)
                                        System.out.print(w + "  ");
                                w = "";                 //initializing variable empty
                        }
                        else
                          w = w + ch;                   //forming a word
                }
        }
}
```

Question 4: **[10]**

Write a program to enter 'n' Telephone numbers in a single dimension array. Search for a telephone number enter by the user. If number found then print the number, otherwise print an appropriate message.

Solution:

```
import java.util.*;
class Linear
 {
        public static void main()
        {
                Scanner sc = new Scanner(System.in);
                int f=0,i,tel[ ],n;
                System.out.println("Enter number of telephone number to be entered");
                n = sc.nextInt();                                       //Storing value of n
                tel=new int[n];                                         //declare array
                System.out.println("Enter Telephone numbers");
```

```
		for(i=0 ; i < n ; i++)
		{
			System.out.print("Enter\n");
			tel[i]=sc.nextInt();
		}
		System.out.println("Enter a telelphone ");
		int num = sc.nextInt();
		for(i=0 ; i < n ; i++)
		{
			if(tel[i]==num)
			{
				f = 1;
				break;		//terminate current loop if condition is true
			}
		}
		if(f==1)
			System.out.println(num);
		else
			System.out.println("search not successful");
	}
}
```

Question 5: **[10]**

Write a program to enter some text and print all consecutive characters from it.

Example: Input string : UNDERSTAND
Output: DE RS ST

Solution:

```
import java.util.*;
class Consecutive
{
	public static void main(String args[ ])
	{
		Scanner sc = new Scanner(System.in);
		String str, w = "";
		int i,len;
		System.out.println("Enter a string");
		str = sc.nextLine();
		str=str.toUpperCase();			// converting into upper case
```

```
		len = str.length( );				//storing length of the string in len
		for(i = 0 ; i < len - 1; i++)
		{
			char ch1 = str.charAt(i);			//copying a character
			char ch2 = str.charAt(i+1);			//copying character next to it
			if(ch1 + 1 == ch2)
				System.out.print(ch1+""+ch2+" ");
		}
	}
}
```

Question 6: **[10]**

Write a program to enter a string. Print the frequency of upper-case characters, lower case characters and digits present in the string.

Solution:

```
import java.util.*;
class Counting
{
	public static void main(String args[ ])
	{
		Scanner sc = new Scanner(System.in);
		String str;
		int i,len,u=0,l=0,d=0;
		System.out.println("Enter a string");
		str = sc.nextLine();
		len = str.length( );		//storing length of the string in len
		for(i = 0 ; i < len - 1; i++)
		{
			char ch = str.charAt(i);
			if(Character.isUpperCase(ch))	//checking for upper case alphabet
				u++;
			else if(Character.isLowerCase(ch))
				l++;
			else if(Character.isDigit(ch))				////checking for digit
				d++;
		}
		System.out.println("Number of upper case alphabets = "+u);
		System.out.println("Number of Lower case alphabets = "+l);
		System.out.println("Number of Digits = "+d);
	}
}
```

Question 7: **[10]**

Write a program to create a single dimensional array of n integers (n is entered by user).

Print only those elements from the array which are Palindrome.
[If reverse of a number is equal to the original number, it is palindrome. Example 121, 12321 etc]

Solution:

```
import java.util.*;
class PalinArray
{
	public static void main()
	{
		Scanner sc = new Scanner(System.in);
		int i,arr[],n,rev = 0,num,rem;
		System.out.println("Enter value of n");
		n = sc.nextInt();
		arr=new int[n];
		System.out.println("Enter Numebrs ");
		for(i=0 ; i < n ; i++)
		{
			System.out.print("Enter\n");
			arr[i]=sc.nextInt();
		}
		for(i=0 ; i < n ; i++)
		{
			rev = 0;
			num = arr[i];
			while(num!=0)
			{
				rem = num%10;            //storing remainder
				rev = rev * 10 + rem;    //reversing the number
				num = num / 10;
			}
			if(arr[i]==rev)
				System.out.println(arr[i])
		}
	}                        //end of main function
}                            //end of class
```

Practice Paper – 3 (Solved)

Computer Application

(Time allotted: One and a half hour)

Maximum Marks: 50

Attempt all questions from **section A** and any four questions from **section B**.

The intended marks for questions or part of questions are given in the brackets [ ].

Section A (10 Marks)

(Attempt all question from this section)

Question1:

Choose the correct answer to the questions from the given options. (Do not write the question, write the correct answer only.) **[10]**

(i) Which of these is not a primitive data type?

(a) int

(b) Boolean

(c) String

(d) float

Solution: Correct option is (c)

(ii) int b = 5/0; which type of error is this?

(a) Run time

(b) Compile time

(c) Syntax

(d) No error

Solution: Correct option is (a)

(iii) Using encapsulation data and methods combines into __________.

(a) package

(b) class

(c) object

(d) None of these

Solution: Correct option is (b)

(iv) Which one is valid array declaration?

(a) int a[10]

(b) int a = new int [10]

(c) int a[ ] = new int[10]

(d) int a[10] = new int [10]

Solution: Correct option is (c)

(v) Which of the following access specifiers makes the member visible to all?

(a) protected
(b) public
(c) private
(d) None

Solution: Correct option is (b)

(vi) char ch[ ] = {'a', 'e', 'i', 'o', 'u'};
System.out.println((int)(ch[ch.length – 5]));

(a) 97
(b) a
(c) 0
(d) None

Solution: Correct option is (a)

(vii) What is value of m from the following code segment:
String v = "aeiou", s = "Computer Application";
int m = v.indexOf(s.charAt(v.indexOf('o')));

(a) 1
(b) 3
(c) –1
(d) p

Solution: Correct option is (c)

(viii) State the return of indexOf( ) function.

(a) boolean
(b) int
(c) char
(d) String

Solution: Correct option is (b)

(ix) Which keyword distinguishes between instance variable and class variable?

(a) class
(b) static
(c) this
(d) final

Solution: Correct option is (b)

(x) Choose the output of the following code segment:

char x = 'A'; int m;
m = (x = 'a') ? 'A' : 'a';
System.out.println("m = " + m);

(a) 97

(b) 65

(c) m = A

(d) m = 97

Solution: Correct option is (d)

Section B (40 Marks)
(Attempt any Four questions from this section)

Question 2: **[10]**

Write a program to enter a string. Convert it into upper case. Count and print vowels separately.

Solution:

```
import java.util.*;
class VowelPrint
{
	public static void main(String args[ ])
	{
		Scanner sc = new Scanner(System.in);
		String str;
		int i, len, a=0, e=0, x=0, o=0, u=0;
		System.out.print("Enter a string");
		str = sc.nextLine();
		str = str.toUpperCase();
		len = str.length();
		for(i=0 ; i<len ; i++)
		{
			char ch = str.charAt(i);
			if(ch == 'A')
				a++;
			else if(ch == 'E')
				e++;
			else if(ch == 'I')
				x++;
			else if(ch == 'O')
				o++;
			else if(ch == 'U')
				u++;
		}
		System.out.println("Number of A = "+a);
		System.out.println("Number of E = "+e);
		System.out.println("Number of I = "+x);
		System.out.println("Number of O = "+o);
		System.out.println("Number of U = "+u);
	}
}
```

Question 3: **[10]**

Write a program to enter an array of 25 elements. Print all prime numbers from the array.

Solution:

```
import java.util.*;
class PrimeArray
{
	public static void main(String args[ ])
	{
		Scanner sc = new Scanner(System.in);
		int arr[] = new int[25], i, c = 0, k, num;
		System.out.println("Enter elements in the array");
		for(i=0 ; i<25 ; i++)
		{
			arr[i] = sc.nextInt( );
		}
		for(i=0 ; i<25 ; i++)
		{
			c = 0;
			num = arr[i];
			for(k=1 ; k<=num ; k++)
			{
				if(num % k == 0)
					c++;
			}
			if(c == 2)
				System.out.println(num + " is a Prime number");
		}
	}
}
```

Question 4: **[10]**

Write a program to accept s sentence and display those words only which starts with vowel

Solution:

```
import java.util.*;
class StartWithVowel
{
	public static void main(String args[])
	{
		Scanner sc = new Scanner(System.in);
		String v = "AEIOUaeiou",str,w = "";
		int i, len;
		System.out.println("Enter a string");
		str = sc.nextLine();
		str = str + " ";
		len = str.length();
		for(i=0 ; i<len ; i++)
```

```
        {
                char ch = str.charAt(i);
                if(ch == ' ')                //is space found
                {
                        char ch1 = w.charAt(0);
                        if(v.indexOf(ch1) >= 0)
                                System.out.print(w + " ");
                        w = "";
                }
                else
                        w = w + ch;
        }
    }
}
```

Question 5: **[10]**

Write a program to 25 telephone number in an array of numeric type and their owner names correspondingly in a string type array. Enter a name to search in the array. If the name present in the array, print the telephone number otherwise print an appropriate message. Use linear search technique.

Solution:

```
import java.util.*;
class Searching
{
    public static void main(String args[ ])
    {
        Scanner sc = new Scanner(System.in);
        String name[] = new String [25],n;
        int arr[] = new int [25],i,flag = 0;
        for(i=0 ; i<25 ; i++)
        {
                System.out.println("Enter a name and Mobile number");
                name[i] = sc.nextLine( );
                arr[i] = sc.nextInt( );
        }
        System.out.println("Enter a name to search");
        n = sc.nextLine( );
        for(i=0 ; i<25 ; i++)
        {
                if(name[i].equalsIgnoreCase(n))
                {
                        flag = 1;
                        break;
                }
        }
        if(flag == 1)
                System.out.println(n + "\t" + arr[i]);
```

```
            else
                System.out.println("Record not found");
        }
}
```

Question 6: **[10]**

Write a program that encodes a word into Piglatin. To translate word into a piglatin word, convert the word into upper case and then place the first vowel of the original word as the start of the new word alongwith the remaining alphabets. The alphabets present before the vowel being shifted towards the end followed by "AY"

Sample Input1 : London
Sample Output1 : ONDONLAY
Sample Input2 : King
Sample Output2 : INGKAY

Solution:

```
import java.util.*;
class PigLatin
{
        public static void main()
        {
                Scanner sc = new Scanner(System.in);
                String str,v = "AEIOU";
                int i,len;
                System.out.println("Enter String ");
                str = sc.nextLine( );
                str = str.toUpperCase();                    //Converting into upper case
                len = str.length();
                for(i=0 ; i<len ; i++)
                {
                        char ch = str.charAt(i);
                        if(v.indexOf(ch)>=0)                //if value of ch is a vowel
                        {
                                String s1 = str.substring(i);
                                String s2 = str.substring(0,i);
                                System.out.println(s1+s2+"AY");
                                break;                      //break from the current loop
                        }
                }
        }
}                                                           //end of class
```

Question 7: **[10]**

Write a program to store 6 elements in an array P, and 4 elements in an array Q and produce a third array, containing all elements of array P and Q. Display the resultant array.

Example: Input/Output:

P[ ]	Q[ ]	R[ ]
4	19	4
6	23	6
1	7	1
2	8	2
3		3
10		10
		19
		23
		7
		8

Solution:

```
import java.util.Scanner;
class MergeArray
{
	public static void main()
	{
		Scanner sc = new Scanner(System.in);
		int P[] = new int[6];
		int Q[] = new int[4];
		int R[] = new int[10];
		int i,k=0;
		System.out.println("Enter elements in P array");
		for(i=0 ; i<6 ; i++)                              //input in array P
			P[i] = sc.nextInt();
		System.out.println("Enter elements in Q array");
		for(i=0 ; i<4 ; i++)                              //input in array Q
			Q[i] = sc.nextInt();
		for(i=0 ; i<6 ; i++)
		{
			R[k]=P[i];                                //shift array P to array R
			k++;
		}
		for(i=0 ; i<4 ; i++)                              //shift array Q to array R
		{
			R[k]=Q[i];
			k++;
		}
		for(i=0 ; i<k ; i++)                              //printing of final array R
		{
			System.out.println(R[i]);
		}
	}
}
```

Unsolved Question Papers

Practice Paper – 1 (Unsolved)

Computer Application

(Time allotted: One and a half hour)

Maximum Marks: 50

Attempt all questions from **section A** and any four questions from **section B.**

The intended marks for questions or part of questions are given in the brackets [ ].

Section A (10 Marks)

(Attempt all question from this section)

Question1:

Choose the correct answer to the questions from the given options. (Do not write the question, write the correct answer only.) **[10]**

(i) Which keyword is used to make a member of class sharable to all objects.

(a) public

(b) static

(c) import

(d) default

(ii) int a[ ] = {2, 4, 6, 8, 12};
System.out.println(a[a.length – 1]);
Output of this code:

(a) 2

(b) 12

(c) 4

(d) None of these

(iii) Which is not a keyword in java?

(a) public

(b) private

(c) protected

(d) friendly

(iv) The block which traps and handle the exception is known as ________

(a) default

(b) try

(c) catch

(d) finally( )

(v) String s[ ] = {“India”, “Japan”, “America”};
Statement to print the length of ‘Japan’:

(a) s[1].length;

(b) s(1).length( );

(c) s[1].length( );

(d) s[2].length( );

(vi) int arr[ ] = {2, 12, 6, 14, 9, 5};
int m = arr[4]%arr[arr.length – 1];
Value stored in m:

(a) 5

(b) 0

(c) 4

(d) 2

(vii) ________ is used to force an exception.

(a) throws

(b) throw

(c) final

(d) try

(viii) Give the output of the following statement:
System.out.println("Computer".endsWith("der"));

(a) false

(b) true

(c) 0

(d) –1

(ix) ______ members can be accessed only in the same class in which they are declared.

(a) private

(b) public

(c) protected

(d) data

(x) String str[ ] = {"Lucknow", "Kanpur", "New Delhi", "Bombay"};
System.out.println(str[0].length( )>str[2].length( ));

(a) true

(b) false

(c) –1

(d) 0

Section B (40 Marks)
(Attempt any four questions from this section)

Question 2: **[10]**

Write a program to enter a string and print it in reverse order.
Input : This is a cat

Output : Cat a is This

Question 3: **[10]**

Write a program to input 'n' integers in an array. Reverse the elements in the same array. Then print the array

Do not use 2nd array.

Question 4: **[10]**

Write a program to enter 10 mobile phone models (String type) and their price (double type) in two different arrays. Input a model of mobile, if it presents in the array, print its price along with model name (Use linear search technique). Otherwise, print an appropriate message.

Question 5: **[10]**

Write a program to input a name. Convert each letter to its opposite case. Print the original and modified name.

Sample input: Rahul Dravid

Sample output: rAHUL dRAVID

Question 6: **[10]**

Write a program to enter an array of 10 elements. Print buzz numbers from the array.

[Numbers which are divisible by 7 or ends with 7 are buzz numbers. Example 175, 207, etc.]

Question 7: **[10]**

Write a program to enter a string. Print the longest word along with its length.

For example : Honesty is the best policy

Longest word: Honesty

Length: 7

Practice Paper – 2 (Unsolved)

Computer Application

(Time allotted: One and a half hour)

Maximum Marks: 50

Attempt all questions from **section A** and any four questions from **section B.**

The intended marks for questions or part of questions are given in the brackets [ ].

Section A (10 Marks)

(Attempt all question from this section)

Question1:

Choose the correct answer to the questions from the given options. (Do not write the question, write the correct answer only.) **[10]**

(i) String str = "3";
System.out.println(Integer.parseInt(str)+ 'a');

(a) 3a

(b) 100

(c) 397

(d) None

(ii) What is return type of startWith( ) function?

(a) int

(b) boolean

(c) String

(d) None

(iii) Conversion of primitive type to its corresponding wrapper class object is called____________

(a) Autoboxing

(b) Unboxing

(c) Type casting

(d) None

(iv) Block that always get executed, no matter which kind of exception is thrown.

(a) finally

(b) default

(c) catch

(d) None

(v) Which package should be imported to use Scanner class

(a) java.util

(b) java.io

(c) java.lang

(d) java.awt

(vi) What is the output of the following code:

```
String s1 = "Amit", s2 = "Amita";
System.out.println(s1. compartTo(s2));
```

(a) −97

(b) −1

(c) 1

(d) 32

(vii) What should be the data type of 'y'?

```
y = (Math.sqrt(16) > 5.0) ? "true" : "false";
```

(a) boolean

(b) String

(c) int

(d) double

(viii)
```
Double n = 15.245;
String s = String.valueOf(n);
char ch = s.charAt(s.indexOf('.') + 1));
System.out.println(ch);
```

(a) 2

(b) 5

(c) 4

(d) 1

(ix) Which library function is used to returns nearest even integer in case of its fractional part is 0.5.

Example: 3.4 = 4.0, 6.5 = 6.0 etc

(a) round ()

(b) random( )

(c) ceil ()

(d) rint( )

(x)
```
int arr[ ] = {1, 4, 8, 6, 12};
System.out.println("sum = " + arr[1] + arr[3]);
```

(a) sum = 10

(b) sum = 9

(c) sum = 46

(d) 46

Section B (40 Marks)

(Attempt any four questions from this section)

Question 2: **[10]**

Write a program to enter number in an array of 10 elements. Print the sum of first 5 elements and product of last five elements.

Question 3: **[10]**

Input a line of text from the user and create a new word formed out of the first letter of each word and convert the new word into uppercase.

Input: Mangoes are delivered after midday

Output: MADAM

Question 5: **[10]**

Write a program to perform binary search on a list of integers given below, to search for an element input by the user, if it is found display the element alongside its position, otherwise display the message "Search element not found"

97, 89, 45, 30, 20, 15, 11, 9, 7, 5

Question 4: **[10]**

Write a program to assign a full path and file name as given below. Using library functions, extract and output the file path, file name and file extension separately as shown.

Input: C:\Users\admin\Pictures\flowers.jpg

Output:

Path: C:\Users\admin\Pictures\

File name: flowers

Extension: jpg

Question 6: **[10]**

Write a program to enter 25 elements in an array. Print sum of those elements only which are multiple of 5.

Question 7: **[10]**

Write a program to enter a word using appropriate function and print the following pattern:

Input: ICSE

Output: I
IC
ICS
ICSE

Practice Paper – 3 (Unsolved)

Computer Application

(Time allotted: One and a half hour)

Maximum Marks: 50

Attempt all questions from **section A** and any four questions from **section B.**

The intended marks for questions or part of questions are given in the brackets [ ].

Section A (10 Marks)

(Attempt all question from this section)

Question1:

Choose the correct answers to the questions from the given options. (Do not write the question, write the correct answer only.) **[10]**

(i) Which keyword is used to make a member of class sharable to all objects?

(a) public
(b) static
(c) import
(d) default

(ii) Given a character array char ch[ ] = {'J', 'A', 'V', 'A'} and an integer a = 2.
What will the output of the following statement?
System.out.println(ch[++a]++);

(a) V
(b) A
(c) B
(d) 3

(iii) What is the output of the following statement?
System.out.println(Character.toUpperCase('T'));

(a) T
(b) true
(c) 'T'
(d) char

(iv) First index of an array is:

(a) 1
(b) 0
(c) −1
(d) length −1

(v) What is the output of the following code segment? System.out.println(57 – '0');

(a) 57
(b) 9

(c) 32

(d) None

(vi) Keyword which informs that an error has occurred in an input/output operation:

(a) throw

(b) throws

(c) catch

(d) try

(vii) Linear search can work on:

(a) Sorted array

(b) Unsorted array

(c) Both sorted and unsorted array

(d) None

(viii) What is the output of the following code segment:

```
double m = 12.5;
String s = String.valueOf(m);
System.out.println(s+2);
```

(a) 14.5

(b) 12.52

(c) 12.0

(d) None

(ix)
```
String s[ ] = {"Lucknow" , "Kanpur", "Kolkata"};
System.out.println(s[0].charAt(s.length));
```

(a) K

(b) k

(c) P

(d) 3

(x) What is the output of the following code segment?

```
String s = "This is a book";
System.out.println(s.lastIndexOf((char)32));
```

(a) space

(b) 9

(c) 15

(d) 4

Section B (40 Marks)
(Attempt any four questions from this section)

Question 2: **[10]**

Write a program to enter a sentence and print the longest word along with its length.

Sample Input: India is a beautiful country
Output: Longest word: beautiful
Length 9

Question 3: **[10]**

Write a program to enter an array of 10 elements. Print factorial of all single digit numbers present in the array.

Question 4: **[10]**

Write a program to input a string in uppercase and print the frequency of each character.

Example: Input: HELLO WORLD

Output:

Characters	Frequency
D	1
E	1
H	1
L	3
O	2
R	1
W	1

Question 5: **[10]**

Write a program to enter an array of n elements. Count and print frequency of all even and odd integers separately.

Question 6: **[10]**

Write a program to store the following names in an array. Enter a name to search in the array. If present print its index otherwise print an appropriate message. Use **binary search** technique.
"Aman", "Amit", "Brajesh", "Danish", "Ekta", "John", "Mayank", "Ritesh", "Vishal", "Zishan"

Question 7: **[10]**

Write a program to enter a string. Convert it into upper case. Print those words only which start and end with the same alphabet.

Input: Amrita and Pooja are good students
Output: AMRITA
STUDENTS

Practice Paper – 4 (Unsolved)

Computer Application

(Time allotted: One and a half hour)

Maximum Marks: 50

Attempt all questions from **section A** and any four questions from **section B.**

The intended marks for questions or part of questions are given in the brackets [ ].

Section A (10 Marks)

(Attempt all question from this section)

Question1:

Choose the correct answer to the questions from the given options. (Do not write the question, write the correct answer only.) **[10]**

(i) Give the output of the following code segment:

```
String n = "Computer Knowledge";
String m = "Computer Application";
System.out.println(n.substring(0, 8).concat(m.substring(9)));
```

(a) Computer Application

(b) ComputerApplication

(c) computer Knowledge

(d) None

(ii) t = Character.isUpperCase('5');

What should be the data type of t?

(a) int

(b) char

(c) boolean

(d) String

(iii) int arr[ ] = {2, 4, 7,12, ,21, 9, 8, 13};

State the last index of the array.

(a) 8

(b) 7

(c) 13

(d) 9

(iv) The output of the following code segment is:

```
String s = "Java is easy to learn";
System.out.println(s.indexOf(s.charAt(s.lastIndexOf(' '))));
```

(a) 4

(b) a

(c) J

(d) y

(v) In java arrays are:

(a) Reference data type

(b) Primitive data type

(c) conditional type

(d) None

(vi) Output of the following code segment:

```
String s = "Examination";
System.out.println(s.startsWith(s.substring(5, s.length( ))));
```

(a) true

(b) false

(c) nation

(d) Examin

(vii) Which feature can be implemented using encapsulation?

(a) Inheritance

(b) Abstraction

(c) Polymorphism

(d) Overloading

(viii) A variable declared in a class using static keyword is __________ variable.

(a) Instance variable

(b) Class variable

(c) Local variable

(d) None

(ix) ______ is used to force an exception.

(a) throws

(b) throw

(c) final

(d) try

(x) What is the output of the following code segment?

```
int arr[ ] = {1, 2, 4, 6, 9, 3, 8}, sum = 0, i;
for(i=1 ; i< arr.length/2 ; i++)
sum = sum + arr[arr.length - i];
System.out.println(sum);
```

(a) 11

(b) 14

(c) 20

(d) 26

Section B (40 Marks)
(Attempt any four questions from this section)

Question 2: **[10]**

Write a program to take input of an array of 10 elements. Print array elements along with the indexes of each element and square of each element in three columns' as following:

Index Number	Element at Index	Square of element
.	.	.
.	.	.
.	.	.

Question 3: **[10]**

Write a program to input any given string to calculate the total number of characters and vowels present in the given string and also reverse the string.

Example: Input: SNOWY

Output:

Total number of characters : 5

Number of vowels : 1

Reverse String : YWONS

Question 4: **[10]**

Write a program to enter 10 positive numbers in a single dimension array. Print factorial of all single digit numbers and sum of digits of remaining numbers.

Question 5: **[10]**

Write a program that encodes a word into Piglatin. To translate word into piglatin word, convert the word into upper case and from the occurrence of the first vowel copy all characters till the end of the word. From beginning of the word copy all characters till the first vowel and shift towards the end followed by "AY".

Sample Input1 : JAVA

Sample Output1 : AVAJAY

Sample Input 2 : PROBLEM

Sample Output 2 :OBLEMPRAY

Question 6: **[10]**

Write a program to enter numbers in an array of 25 elements. Input a number and find and print the frequency of that number in the array.

Question 7: **[10]**

Write a program to accept the names of 10 cities in a single dimension string array and their STD (Subscriber Trunk Dialing) codes in another single dimension integer array. Search for a name of a city input by the user in the first list. If found display Search Successful and print the name of the city along with its STD code else display the message Search Unsuccessful.

Practice Paper – 5 (Unsolved)

Computer Application

(Time allotted: One and a half hour)

Maximum Marks: 50

Attempt all questions from **section A** and any four questions from **section B.**

The intended marks for questions or part of questions are given in the brackets [ ].

Section A (10 Marks)

(Attempt all question from this section)

Question1:

Choose the correct answer to the questions from the given options. (Do not write the question, write the correct answer only.) **[10]**

(i) Process of wrapping of data members and member functions into a single unit is called encapsulation. What is the single unit is called?

(a) Object

(b) Class

(c) Abstraction

(d) None

(ii) When you pass an array to a method, the method receives ___________

(a) A copy of the array

(b) A copy of the first element

(c) The reference of the array

(d) The length of the array

(iii) int arr[ ] = new int[0];
System.out.println(arr.length);
What is the result when the following code will be complied and executed ?

(a) Compilation error

(b) Run time error (program will terminate with some error message)

(c) 0

(d) None

(iv) Which one is invalid comment in java?

(a) // comment

(b) /*comment*/

(c) */comment*/

(d) None

(v) In java, a group of classes is called:

(a) Objects

(b) Encapsulation

(c) Package

(d) Array

(vi) Which will legally declare, construct and initialize an array?

(a) int a( ) = {1, 2, 3, 4};

(b) int a[ ] = (2, 3, 5, 6);

(c) int a[ ] = {2, 1, 6, 9, 8};

(d) int a[ ] = {1, 2.5, 8, 12};

(vii) Which of these method of string class can be used to test to strings for equality?

(a) isequal( )

(b) isequals( )

(c) equals( )

(d) equalsTo

(viii) String class is defined in which of these packages?

(a) java.lang

(b) java.util

(c) java.io

(d) java.string

(ix) In java how many bytes are consumed by the following array in memory ?
int arr[ ] = new int [15];

(a) 15

(b) 20

(c) 30

(d) 60

(x) What is the output of the following code segment?
String str = "Hello World";
System.out.println(str.indexOf('h'));

(a) 0

(b) 1

(c) −1

(d) None

Section B (40 Marks)
(Attempt any four questions from this section)

Question 2: **[10]**

Write a program to print consecutive letters placed next to each other. Also print the frequency of such occurance.

Input Text : Abacus operates abstantially.
Output : Ab op ab st
Number of Words : 4

Question 3: **[10]**

Write a program in java to accept the name and contact number of 25 people in two separate arrays. The program should ask the user for a contact number and search for it in the contact number array using the linear Search technique. If the number is found, then the corresponding name is displayed otherwise a proper error message is displayed.

Question 4: **[10]**

Write a program to enter a string and print * at place of vowels.

Example:

Input : Java is easy to learn.
Output : J*v* *s **sy t* l**rn.

Question 5: **[10]**

Write a program to store 8 elements in array P, and 5 elements in array Q and produce a third array R, containing first element from array P then second element from array Q, and so on. When all elements of an array has transferred, transfer all elements of another array into R. Print array R.

Example:

P[ ]	**Q[ ]**	**R[ ]**
4	19	4
6	23	19
1	7	6
2	8	23
3	5	1
10		7
11		2
14		8
		3
		5
		10
		11
		14

Question 6: **[10]**

Special words are those words which start and end with the same letter.

Example: EXISTENCE, COMIC, WINDOW, etc.

Palindrome words are these words which read the same from left to right and vice – versa.

Example: ARORA, MALYALAM, MADAM etc.

All palindromes are special words but all special are not palindrome.

Write a program to enter a word, check and print whether the word is a palindrome or only special word only.

Question 7: **[10]**

Write a program to enter a word. Convert it into upper case. Print the following pattern from the word:

Input : Hello
Output : O
LO
LLO
ELLO
HELLO

Practice Paper – 6 (Unsolved)

Computer Application

(Time allotted: One and a half hour)

Maximum Marks: 50

Attempt all questions from **section A** and any four questions from **section B.**

The intended marks for questions or part of questions are given in the brackets [ ].

Section A (10 Marks)

(Attempt all question from this section)

Question1:

Choose the correct answer to the questions from the given options. (Do not write the question, write the correct answer only.) **[10]**

(i) What is the return type of the replace(char, char) function:

(a) char

(b) boolean

(c) String

(d) int

(i) If int arr[ ] = {4,7,12, 8, 9, 10}; what is the value of p?
p = arr[arr.length – 1] + arr[0] * arr[1];

(a) 12

(b) 38

(c) 28

(d) 48

(iii) Which keyword distinguishes between instance variable and class variable?

(a) class

(b) static

(c) this

(d) final

(iv) String s = "MISSISSIPPI";
System.out.println(s.indexOf('S')+s.lastIndexOf('s'));

(a) –1

(b) 1

(c) 2

(d) –2

(v) Element num[10] is which element of the array?

(a) 11th

(b) 9th

(c) 12th

(d) 8th

(vi) Visibility of ___________ variables are limited to the function, in which they are declared.

(a) Instance

(b) Arguments

(c) Class

(d) Local

(vii) compareTo( ) method returns:

(a) 1

(b) false

(c) int type value

(d) true

(viii) Which is the wrapper class for int data type?

(a) Int

(b) Integer

(c) integer

(d) None

(ix) Process of conversion from wrapper class to its respective primitive data type is called________

(a) Autoboxing

(b) Unboxing

(c) Encapsulation

(d) Method calling

(x) Block that always get executed no matter which kind of exception is thrown:

(a) finally( )

(b) default

(c) catch

(d) None

Section B (40 Marks)
(Attempt any Four questions from this section)

Question 2: **[10]**

Write a program to enter a name. Print it as per the following example:
Input : Sachin Ramesh Tendulkar
Output: S.R. Tendulkar

Question 3: **[10]**

Write a program to enter numbers in two different array having 10 elements in both. Check and print whether both arrays are identical or not.(order of elements are important)

For example:
Let P[ ] = {2, 4, 7, 9} and Q[ ] = {2, 4, 7, 9} are identical arrays.
P[ ] = {2, 5, 7, 9} and Q[ ] = {2, 4, 6, 9} are not identical arrays.
P[ ] = {2, 5, 7, 9} and Q[ ] = {2, 7, 5, 9} are not identical arrays.

Question 4: **[10]**

Write a program to enter a word. Convert it into upper case then arrange its alphabets in alphabetical order (a to z).
Print the original and new word.

Example:
Input : India
Output : Original word : INDIA
Word after sorting : ADIIN

Question 5: **[10]**

Write a program to input a String array, containing 10 words, in Uppercase. Print those words only which start and end with vowels.

Question 6: **[10]**

Write a program to enter an array. Copy this into another array in reverse order. Finally, print the sum of elements of both arrays.

Example:
A[ ] contains : 2, 8, 3, 7, 4, 5
B[ ] contains : 5, 4, 7, 3, 8, 2
Ouput : 7 12 10 10 12 7

Question 7: **[10]**

Write a program to enter a string. Convert it into upper case. Reprint the string by replacing "The" with "THAT".
Sample Input: The book is on the table
Sample Output: THAT BOOK IS ON THAT TABLE

Practice Paper – 7 (Unsolved)

Computer Application

(Time allotted: One and a half hour)

Maximum Marks: 50

Attempt all questions from **section A** and any four questions from **section B.**

The intended marks for questions or part of questions are given in the brackets [ ].

Section A (10 Marks)

(Attempt all question from this section)

Question1:

Choose the correct answer to the questions from the given options. (Do not write the question, write the correct answer only.) **[10]**

(i) What is the return type of substring ( ) method?

(a) boolean

(b) String

(c) char

(d) int

(ii) State the data type of p.

p = "A" + 2.5 * 2;

(a) double

(b) String

(c) int

(d) None

(iii) Which is the default java package?

(a) java.awt

(b) java.io

(c) java.lang

(d) java.util

(iv) What is the index of element 'i' in the following array:

char ch[ ] = {'a', 'e', 'i', 'o', ''u}

(a) 3

(b) 2

(c) 1

(d) None

(v) Give the output of the following code:

System.out.println("Better".startsWith("Bet"));

(a) true

(b) false

(c) Bet

(d) None

(vi) The block which traps and handles the exception is known as________

(a) default

(b) try

(c) final

(d) try

(vii) System.out.println("A" + 2.5 * 2);

(a) A2.52

(b) A5.0

(c) A2.5*2

(d) None

(viii) Give output of the following Java code :

```
String str = "JAVA";
char ch = str.charAt(7/2);
int as = ch;
System.out.println((char)as);
```

(a) 65

(b) A

(c) a

(d) None

(ix) Act of combining data and its associated function into a single unit is known as __________

(a) Encapsulation

(b) Polymorphism

(c) Inheritance

(d) Data abstraction

(x) Corresponding wrapper class of char data type is:

(a) Char

(b) Character

(c) char

(d) None of these

Section B (40 Marks)
(Attempt any four questions from this section)

Question 2: **[10]**

Write a program to enter a string. Reprint the string so that each vowel is replaced by its next vowel.

Sample Input : It is an Umbrella

Sample Output : Ot os en Ambrille

Question 3: **[10]**

Write a program to enter numbers in an array of 10 elements of integer type. Print sum of all even numbers and sum of all odd numbers in two separate lines.

Question 4: **[10]**

Write a program to enter a string and perform the shifting of alphabets (only) in circular fashion according to key.

Input String : Zoo
Input key : 2
String After Shirt : Bqq

Question 5: **[10]**

Write a program to enter an array of 10 elements. Print the sum of all elements present at even indexes.

Question 6: **[10]**

Write a program to enter a string. Print the word which has highest number of vowels.

Question 7: **[10]**

Write a program to enter n Telephone numbers in a single dimension array and their owners in another array. Search for a telephone number enter by the user. If number found then print the number along with owner name, otherwise print an appropriate message

www.ingramcontent.com/pod-product-compliance
Ingram Content Group UK Ltd.
Pitfield, Milton Keynes, MK11 3LW, UK
UKHW061705190726
13853UKWH00008B/2409

9 789355 563286